T0194049

Love
Me
LIKE YOU
Loved
Them

Love Me LIKE YOU Loved Them

IF GOD BE FOR YOU

REVERAL L. YEARGIN

LOVE ME LIKE YOU LOVED THEM
IF GOD BE FOR YOU

iUniverse books may be ordered through booksellers or by contacting:

iUniverse
1663 Liberty Drive
Bloomington, IN 47403
www.iuniverse.com
1-800-Authors (1-800-288-4677)

Because of the dynamic nature of the Internet, any web addresses or links contained in this book may have changed since publication and may no longer be valid. The views expressed in this work are solely those of the author and do not necessarily reflect the views of the publisher, and the publisher hereby disclaims any responsibility for them.

Any people depicted in stock imagery provided by Getty Images are models, and such images are being used for illustrative purposes only. Certain stock imagery © Getty Images.

ISBN: 978-1-5320-7004-4 (sc)
ISBN: 978-1-5320-7005-1 (e)

Print information available on the last page.

iUniverse rev. date: 03/08/2019

CONTENTS

BOOK REVIEW/ RECOMMENDATION:

I found extreme pleasure in reading Yeargin's first volume of "Beacon of Hope". It reminds readers that all successes begin with hope; from hoping to rise each morning to hoping others see us in favorable ways. Through the book we realize hope-combined with faith-is a guiding principle that lights our path as we move through life.

James A. Dula, PhD
Executive Director
Niaiman Choices Inc
"Where dreams come true"

DEDICATION

This poetic project is being dedicated to people from all across the United States of America and around the world. I have written many poetic letters about mine and their lifestyles. I have gathered opinions from people of all walks of life and they have given me their honest reviews about each poem. I would be remiss if I didn't thank them all once again for being totally honest with their statements. This entire body of work would not be possible without the inspiration of God the Father, Jesus Christ, and the Holy Ghost. There is a special crowd of people who have pushed me into publishing this miraculous poetic project.

INTRODUCTION

Welcome to MiraculousMinistries.org and (Miraculouspoetry.com), Volume II

It has been a joy to write through the inspiration of the Holy Spirit in obedience to the call of Jesus Christ. Each of these poetic letters is an inspiration of people, places and things. It is being presented to the best of my knowledge and the industry standard. I want nothing less than to give these messages to the world in the highest form and the God we serve would want nothing less than the best.

Over the past 20-years, I have been writing in and out of season and I pray that each letter will become your answer in your time of need. I have made many friends thus far and please allow me to say thank you for becoming my newest friend.

Before, I tried to write any of this material, I sought the Lord Jesus Christ in prayer. And, I pray that you take out a moment to pray for a complete understanding of what you are about to read. These words have been written for the clarity of our views and viewpoints that are connected to our public and private lives. All of us are searching for answers to our many questions and none of us know where to search to find the answers. This collection of poetic letters is just another way of gaining peace of mind of those things that we don't understand. My prayer is that we study this body of work repeatedly, and not look at this collection of words as another cluster of sentences that mean nothing. At some point, we must move past rejecting all wisdom, knowledge, and understanding, and embrace those paths that have been set before us in love.

Learn all you can while you can and be all that you can be within the timeframe you have on this earth. One thing I would not do is to say those things that are detrimental to my continued growth and your search for clarity. At all cost, I am trying to reach the next generations and at the same time encourage our present generation to embrace progressiveness. If you have questions in your mind don't shut out another avenue that could bless you.

Become an open book and empower yourself above the rest, what you do for yourself is for you and no one else!

SPECIAL THANKS

I would like to give a Special thanks to my family, the Yeargin's; the late Horace Sr., and Naomi, Johnny, Beverly, Ron, Horace. Jr., Clarence and Gwen, Jennifer and Carlos. Monique Smith and family, Uncle Jimmy and Family, Uncle Bill and family, Uncle Brock and Family, Lynn, My cousine, My nieces; Erin. Lauryn, Cortlyn, Stephanie, Jazmin, Ashley, Amber, and Cassandra. My Nephews; Mr. Ryan, Nicholas, Dominique, and Chris. Ms. Regina Lamb, My only son Reggie, Ms. Ethel Taylor, Nicole Yeargin, Wesley Mountain, Janis Brunson, Pastor William's Sr., and Jr of Saint Paul Church Family, Carl, Freddie Hall, Lorenzo, Parris, Raymond Portis, Ralph Page, Eugene Grant and Dashaun Lanham, Seat Pleasant City Council, Geno Johnson, Terry Brooks, Johnny Dodd, Lewis Oliver, Angela Jenkins, Jay Ford, Darryl Davis, Linda Vannall, Patricia Page and all of my political friends from around the world.

"Love Me Like You Loved Them!"

Is it possible to love me and be honorable towards me just like you have loved them?
I have done more than any human being could have ever dreamed of doing for you!
My love for you is automatic and it will only grow stronger if we could commune together!
The strength you have come from me and whenever you get tired I am there to put you to sleep!
I saw you chasing them and I saw you begging for their affection, and deep inside of my heart I still love you!

I like taking long walks in the park and staying long after dark!
Whenever you get the chance could we come together and talk just like we just met?
Last night when you turned your back towards me I didn't get out of bed to sleep on the couch!
I did like a real lover would do I stayed there and watched over you!
Then early this morning I touched you with my fingers of love so we could try once again!

Are you thinking of me as much as I am thinking of you?
Fresh flowers are my favorite and to get one from a loved one is the greatest!
I am not the type of lover you could buy, but it will be nice to get something every now and then!
The food that you enjoy I grew it and the way you like riding in your car I made it!
The clothes you are wearing came from me and the desire you have to live was a gift from me!

Can we fast and pray together and become closer and closer like a real couple?
No flesh shall ever glory in my sight but my love for your soul made me give my very life!
I did not stay in the grave, My love for you brought me back in three days!
I am here whenever you need me and I will be there whenever you feel like no one really cares!
Just show me that you love me more than you love them!

Thank you for loving me and treating me like your closest lover and best friend!
Although the days are long and the nights are dark, there is no need for you to have fear inside of your heart!
I would never leave you nor will I forsake you, My love for you will last forever!
Call my name before you call them and you will never call their name again!
My Agape love is more than enough to keep you until we meet again!

"501 Heavens Boulevard"

There is a place high up in the heavens and if I could get there I would ask God a thousand questions
The first question is this "Why did You take me out of heaven and placed me in this place called earth?"
The second question is this "What does going down has to do with getting up?"
The third question is this "When will You come back and make all of my enemies my footstool?"
The fourth question is this "What kind of place are You preparing for me after I die?"

By falling down on my knees in prayer I am expecting to hear the voice of God inside of my soul
If I have all of the questions there has to be a God who is sitting on high who has all of the answers
I am not the first person to have these insecurities and if the world keep on turning I would not be the last
As a blood bought child of God I have more than the right to inquire about these matters of my soul
Until I hear from God I will remain content without saying something that would get me banded from heaven

So many souls have abandon the Salvation plan of the Lord because in this day and time they feel that they have a greater plan

Men maybe healthy today but who will step in and save their sin sick souls on tomorrow?

Man has to ability to buy an assortment of things but why is it not possible for a man to buy good health?

As fast as our lives have started they all could end even faster and without giving a clear explanation

The Bible clearly states the pleasures of heaven and according to them it is going to be a lovely place

In less than 130 years our eternal fate would be determined but in less than a minute we could secure it forever

Would you love to sit at the feet of Jesus Christ and glorify God His Father for saving your soul from a burning hell

Nothing is more important than your soul and that one fact should never be changed by anyone or anything

In short that is what all of our struggling is all about and Jesus Christ gave His life so that we could be saved

Be at peace my brother and be at rest my sister for the Lord has prepared for all of us heavens best

Every great relationship starts with a conversation and before we know it the conversation has ended

Make your request known unto the Lord and never waver in your faith because the God we serve is faithful

The issues of this day may be dark but the darkness of this day is the start of a greater tomorrow

Allow the glory of God to carry you to the place that no man has ever visited and when you get there fall down on your face

Nothing is greater than to hear our God say "Well done my good and faith servant inter into My rest!"

"A Place Called Rest"

There is a place that no man has ever been and because of God
I have found a treasured place of rest
I can go there whenever I feel weary from well doing because in
due season I shall reap if I faint not
All of us desire a place of rest after we have been through our
storms to free our minds and to comfort our souls
These old feeble bodies have to rest for a moment, a minute, a
hour, or for a longer extended period of time
You would not be the person you are without the proper rest and
you and I know that is the truth

In the midst of my storms I cannot feel a thing because the God
I serve is bigger than my trials
My test may turn into a trial and my trials could turn into a
burden but none of them are bigger than my God
Having a heart of flesh is the greatest and with this heart I can
feel the Spirit of the Lord moving inside of me
Wherever the Lord is there is liberty and to know that God is
here is comforting to my soul
I have peace in the city and peace in the field and heavenly rest
whenever I get weary

My hope and trust is in a God who knew me before I knew
myself
Nothing about my past, present, or future, is foreign to the God
who create all mankind

When my heart needs rest I seek the heart fixer and when my mind is confused I can study the Word of God to get renewed
God help my feet whenever I am standing on them and please at the same time strengthen my lower back
My God is with me in the good and the bad, the happy and the sad; and He knows when I need some rest

I can be on my job and have rest and at the same time do my job and finish way before quitting time
My labor is unto the Lord and not unto man; I may work for them but my heart is in God's hands
They said I was a good worker and a devoted employee but God said I was blessed in the city as well as in the field
I like to work but I love coming home to be with my family were I am blessed to see the fruits of my labor
When the world is giving me more than I am getting at home something is unbalanced inside of my house

Jesus Christ is here, there, and everywhere, the peace of the Savior is readily available to anyone with the faith to ask
The Lord has promised to never leave us and to never forsake us
If you are confused with this life I dare to say you have put your trust in your flesh
God can give anything to you but if there is sin dwelling inside of your members simply pray for your forgiveness
Can you imagine our spirits sitting in heavenly places and experiencing eternal rest for our weary souls?

"A Thousand Words"

What a challenging statement to have so early in the morning for it is pressing upon my gift to finally be revealed
One word after the other and another thought that means more than just meaningless ideas
Creating what has never been created and expanding the thoughts of men, women, and children all around the world
If you had a thousand words at your leisure how would you formulate them to ensure maximum impact?
Or would you simply say from a empty vessel they don't exist for what else could a unlearned person say?

This literary offering when finished will conclude with about a thousand words
Some will be quick to the point while others are intentionally slowed to make you think before you react
It has been said millions of times if you want to hide something just write it in a book
This is the key to success and as long as the world turns the smartest people will rule the illiterate people of the world
The educated don't want you to become educated because when you do they may have to work for you

Do you really think everyone is happy to see me publishing book after book without repeating literary hooks?
These offerings will become the social standard because they are filled with righteousness and wisdom from God

God has a way of dumbfounding the wise and making the lesser far greater than the wise

When you play with words those words will play on you but if you speak the truth the truth will in turn speak for you

Look I'm trying with all of my might to make these thousand words come to life

They say "a picture is worth a thousand words" and I say a letter with fifty two part sentences is about a thousand words

There is a powerful, thoughtful, caring, individual living within you and thank God you know it too

You are more than a thought you are the next genius to walk on the face of this earth

I'm wondering why is it so hard for you to accept the credit for what you will become and for who you are right now?

There comes a time when you have to speak your mind and tell the world which way to turn

Whatever you say out of your mouth originated from your heart and hopefully you took in account the consequences

A thousand words is not a small feat to achieve but for some people it could render them helpless

Thinking is the key to fulfilling your goals and the more you think them through the greater they will become to you

Say a thousand words in any presentation and watch everyone in the room stand up and applaud your dissertation

With a thousand words at your pleasure and having the gift of gab will now open doors you never thought could ever open

Knowing the definition of one word is ok but having the ability to manipulate a thousand definitions consecutively is powerful

Every writer must take in affect the effect of their words will have on audiences seen and unseen

Always be at your best when speaking to anyone and that confidence only comes through your conversations
You will always be smarter than some people and better informed than others but never wiser than your elders
Where there is a thought there is an question and when there is an issue it is people like yourself who will solve them

God created words to properly identify who, where, and what things are because we needed clarification he didn't
What you say could be interpreted incorrectly and what you don't say has a meaning of its own
People will try to put words into your mouth and unequivocally determine your definitions whether right or wrong
Say what you desire within your own heart and stand firm whenever they try to define your intentions
You should know what you desire to say before you attempt to speak and say them without being interpreted as being weak

Set your own path without apologies and make them respect your gifts by what your offering and not by default
Simply writing a sentence shows your ability to structure words into multiple fashions to say normal or abnormal things
Somebody has to say something in order for someone else to respond to their request
There are A thoughts, B thoughts, and C thoughts, A is the first thing you think, B is the second, and C is being silent
Never say the first thing that comes into your mind because that statement could cause some embarrassment

Every miraculous work has some flaws and every dream must have a dreamer who seeks to fulfill their dreams
Close your eyes with confidence and open them with the expectation of becoming that which you dreamt of

If you had the heart to speak then you should have the desire to reach for them
Everything has a beginning and in this life they will have an ending but just know the middle is worth the journey
Show me what's living deep inside of you and I will gladly render my thoughts, my encouragement, and my support

With only a thousand words at my pleasure speak them as plainly as possible, clearly as you could, and with power
We have the knowledge to speak a thousand words without any profanity, racial epithets, or discrimination
Knowledge opens windows to the world and speak words of expectations, salutations, infatuations, and congratulations
Whatever they ask simply say in return words of greater meanings, higher thoughts, and of infinite wisdoms
Now you have more than a thousand words to say so please don't become speechless whenever they ask you to speak

"An Old Stack of Love Letters"

All we have ever made were promises that neither they or I could ever keep
This may seem old fashion to some when in fact writing to someone in your own hand writing is more intimate
From start to finish the entire letter is personal and no one else could phantom what your thoughts are
You could try to flatter them with your silliness or you could take a serious route and speak to their heart?
Just be reminded that whatever you write on those slips of paper could and will be held against you forever

At first their words sounded so sweet and in return I gave them just as much to think
First and foremost I told them just how much I admired their thoughtfulness for those intimate words came from the bottom of my heart
We went back and fourths for months before we took a break from continuous letter swapping
Even now we refer to those love letters of our past and of how we wanted those moments to last
Well, time moves on and having a pen pal who actually cares is priceless

One after the other they fell into my mailbox and before the night was over I had sent them back a sweeter response
Why do the best relationships last longer when the two persons never physically touch?
Every loving relationship started with a conversation either written in word or with a verbal gesture
Along with those special words we also would include a smiley face or another cartoon character
Do you have a special person that you are secure with sending personal thoughts through the mail?

Sometimes we would laugh through our words and other times our letters would be blurred because of our tears
Each letter that we sent would be filled with passions and when opened a fresh flowery smell would rush from the pages
Our days were filled with quiet moments reminiscing about the words that we had written on empty pieces of paper
No pencil or slip of paper were safe around my home because I have plenty of words to send to my lover
I knew I was doing a great job because of the timely responses I was getting from my distant lover

Suddenly the love letters stopped and from their last response I think they have moved on
I have heard of falling out of love but have you ever heard of running out of intimate words to say?
As you can read I still have words to speak but my problem is having a forwarding address to send them to
I wanted us to communicate forever but unless our words are fruitful our letter writing is over
The smartest people in the world would write a love letter to themselves and wait by the mailbox for its return

"As Promised"

What can we do when all we are doing is waiting?
Others are planning their futures and all of their plans are coming into fruition
We have made plans only to see them fall into the ditch and land us back at zero
We could have taken the easy road but what good would that be when we are seeking excellence
Where is the love that was promised to me way before I came into being?

If someone promised you something they must have the ability to bring it to pass
They must have the keys to my success and they can open any door they have promised to open
At their call my issues are no more and everything I were promised is within my grasp
Change is a good thing when our situations are outside of our reach
If God did not promise it I don't recommend sitting around waiting for a change to come

I am going to sit right here and do nothing until my change comes
Faith without works is dead and works without faith is also dead
With only a mustard seed of faith you could move any mountain out of your way

Have you ever made a promise that you could not fulfill and everybody became mad at you?
What are you doing to insure your half of the promise?

After you get it will you thank the source whom brought it to pass?
Name me one thing that you thought of and then had the power to bring it to pass?
Now that I have it within my grasp I can do with it as I please
A promise is no longer a promise when what you have asked for is in your possession
I don't have to call on God until I have another issue, problem, or circumstance?

When we receive our promises from God we really shouldn't rest, but rather become better
Now that we are recipients of these gifts from heaven these experiences should make us grateful
Please note that everybody does not receive the blessings from God because they are not His children
Yes, His mercy reigns on the just and the unjust but those heavenly promises are not for the sinner
God has promised us many things and most of us are not aware of them

Have you ever had somebody to make you a promise and they actually fulfilled it?
Have you ever made a promise that you knew you could not fulfill?
To make a promise and not perform it is called a lie
Never put your word on the line because your word is your bond

We have been given some power to do something wonderful for somebody else

Ask and it shall be given, seek and you shall find, knock and the doors shall be opened unto you

When we do our part as commanded by God then anything we ask for shall be given

Only a thief and a robber would want something for free when nothing in this world is free

Why don't you promise God to be obedient and finally become a humbled servant?

It is just as easy to do what is right as it is to do something that is wrong

I promise to write the truth the whole truth and nothing but the truth so help me God

Because of my humble heart and my belief in Jesus Christ, I want nothing but the best for you

Every word that I have place on these blank sheets of paper will follow me all the way to my grave

I desire to leave a legacy that would redefine the way generations will walk, think, and live for God

At my judgment God will open every book and judge everything; and every word that I have said

Because of your faith God did as promised and that is exactly what He promised to do

The Lord said, "Heaven and earth shall pass away before a jot or tear of My Word comes back void!"

We could be in the ditch with all of our business in the streets, and God is still able to save us

Rest assured that nothing this world could ever do has the power to undo anything God have promised
On the day Jesus Christ was crucified He said "Father forgive them for they knew not what they do!"

Then Jesus promised to willingly lay down His own life and return back to life in three days
Our Lord has gone away to prepare a place and where He is there we shall be also
Jesus may have gone away but He promised to come back again
In a moment and in a tinkling of an eye our Savior shall crack the sky just as He promised

"Ask and It Shall Be Given"

What would you have God to do and if asked could you explain the entire prayerful process? What would be the first thing you do when asking God for something He may not instantly approve? What would be the second thing you do after the first request failed to be approved? What would be the fourth thing you do if the first request went through? What would be the last thing you do after the first request was granted and your humbled prayer request is not a part of you?

When consulting God what should be your posture, or do you think it truly matters? Who is God and who is the creator for in the beginning was God and the worlds were without form. Who says a prayer and who answers them and who is sitting high and looking low? God is in everything and everywhere and before you even thought about its God knew what you were thinking. If, we never ask God, he is not obligated to answer and when we ask anything in His Name He Will answer in due season.

I heard a still small voice saying unto me "What would you have me to do?"
If, I heard Him then you can hear Him because some strange way you can hear everything else without a problem. Do you hear me speaking through these words then you can hear God because it is Jesus Christ who is writing them? I did not create them, and I cannot ordain them for they are placed within my hands for only

a season. Get them while you can and when they are gone they are not coming back this way again.

What gift from a man would make you happy or should every gift from God make you a better person? Gifts are given without repentance and because God saw fit to give you something special you should be eternally grateful. The words that I write are a gift and the books you see are a collection of gifts. What God is giving to me I, in turn give to you and will you treat them as a gift or a miraculous gift from God. This could be the answer to all your questions and God has a way of moving in mysterious ways.

The Word of God tells us what, how, when, and why, we should seek Him first before we seek anything else.
A- set yourself in a humble posture and ask God for everything you desire to receive.
S- use your mouth to say what you mean and hold God to every word He has said
K- know that God has a plan for your life and you must get in the way and allow God to work His perfect work
It is as simple as that and because God Is Who He Is we can become everything He desires for us to be.

"Bless Me Once More"

The last time you spoke over my life everything you said had an instant effect on the way I view the world
Before I were scared of everything but now everything has been placed under my feet
They had me so fearful I could not speak my heart or voice what was in my mind
Confidence I had none and courage would not be my friend because the devil had me all shook up
Today I thank God for "A Beacon of Hope" for it has inspired me to reach for the highest of mountains

I appreciate the gifts God has given to all the world and I really thank God for using only the humble
God had to know that I was financially unable to pay you for blessing my life
You did not ask me for anything but you did allow God to use your gift in a miraculous way
I have always been amazed of how the Lord could sit in heavenly places and still find the time to bless my life
Who am I to command the God of all creation to come all the way from heaven and to bless a wretch like me?

You said a lot of things and some of your words were spot on with most of my intimate dreams
Yes they hurt me and yes they said some awful things and no I did not wish the same things to happen to them

Once I dreamed of helping beaten and broken human beings
because I never wanted to see another person hurt
God has given me some tough skin and an emotional level that is
far beyond my own selfish needs

Some people act weird when it comes to the things of God but
you are the most normal minister I know
You have to constantly study the Word of God to do the things
you do and to speak nothing but the truth
I want to be a witness of the truth that you were sent from God
because my entire life has changed for the better
I am falling in love with God all over again and I am not ashamed
to tell the world about it
Thank you for giving and not taking; and thank you for being a
blessing and not a curse

Last night I prayed for the minister who blessed me like no
other and truthfully I meant every last word of it
I prayed so hard that warm tears fell from my eyes and my
emotions were full of the joy of the Lord
God had to know that I needed someone to touch and agree with
those things He wanted to do for me
All of my needs include my visions and dreams; and another
blessed minister to put a stamp of approval on them
Now I can smile and now I can laugh because Salvation has come
into my life to stay.

"Bless Those Who Blesses Me"

On a cold and blissful night without another person in sight my kids and I are locked out of our apartment

Our lives have turned from bad to worse soon after we came home from church

I knew our housing arrangement was not as it should have been but in reality whose is

I cannot do no more than the Lord allows and try to be the greatest single parent at the same time

He said he would love me and my kids for the rest of our days and be to me the man I have prayed for

The question is how did I get into this ditch and now me and my kids are out in the street

All of my friends are nice as long as I don't need anything but it is two in the morning and we are locked out

Something is coming over me and I cannot cry or shed a tear because of it, I have to be stronger than this situation

Where does a single mom go at two AM with her two kids and no place to turn in for the night?

I could grab a blanket and sleep under a tree but how would I comfort my two kids?

I could go without eating and sleep in my same clothes but what would I tell my kids when they are just kids
I could go without being loved and treated like a lady but my kids are not that emotional stable
How could I charge my cell phone to call for help and wake up somebody who is close to me and my kids
This homeless situation is right here and I cannot run away from it
Obviously, I have been with several men and none of them cared to love me after we had our kids

All of this is my fault for not guarding my heart and because I allowed boys acting like a man into my life
I had help in making my babies but they didn't feel the need to stay and help raise their own children
In reality I am scared and I don't know where to turn for help other than the church
I know God will make a way and I know He would never leave me or forsake me but where is God when I need Him?
God must have saw all of this coming because He is Omni present and the Word of God says God really cares

I need to turn to somebody for help and I doubt it would be in the arms of another boy posing as a man
I don't care for the affection of a woman and I feel totally confident in my personality to remain strong
Some people are pushed into a worse situation than they had because they did not consult with the Lord
We may have to find some kind of shelter for the night but in the morning I am looking for God to show up
My relationship with God is sure and my heart is pure, God can and God will get my family into a place called home

Were you warm and cozy last night and did you say a prayer for struggling mothers who really need some help?
I am sobbing inside and out and my feet are hurting because I am carrying my daughter in my arms
Thank God that my son is old enough to walk and the he cannot feel the reality of our homeless situation
I pray that the security guard does not come into work early because this is the only place I could find to sleep
It is raining and all of our rain stuff is locked away and we are stuck inside of this guard shack for the night

There is no need to worry because worrying cannot change a thing just pray that we make it until morning
This is not a good situation to be in when you are a single mother with two kids and no place to live
Lord, I am trusting in You to keep us safe and Lord please don't let nothing bad happen to me and my kids
There is no place to wash our faces and brush our teeth before we turn in for a peaceful night of heavenly rest
I surely could use one of those blessings right now and after I get it I would not have a problem with saying thank you.

"Catch Me If You Can"

One day I'm going to fall, and the entire world knows it's not a pretty scene at all. After, exerting myself I'm left gasping for my breath and unless you catch me I'm totally helpless. Starting out my day I'm exactly like every other human being but the problem comes when I'm trying to finish. Have you ever run out of energy in the middle of your day and thought to yourself "Who's going to catch me?" We all have deficiencies to manage and at times we do over exert our physical limits and end up flat on our faces.

Why me and not you, could this be treated or healed completely, or is God not caring for me like He said He would? Tears cannot help me, and my fears will never stop me from giving it my all. Blinded by an ailment that I never saw coming but deep inside of me it will never cripple my will to succeed. The facts are in and the odds are stacked against me for with this situation I am even more determined to win. Don't cry for me because I've seen my own tears but rather cheer for me as I conquer my fears.

Like this blank sheet of paper no one can predict the outcome but, in the end, there are words bigger than my imagination. Time after time I have pushed mind to write things my past cannot support, and this is another attempt at greatness. I know they are in my mind for all the world to see and with another intricate thought they suddenly appear unto me. See, I told you God had given me the gift of writing and look again for these collections of words are so exciting. Catch these next thoughts for they all are running back and fourths as they speak from deep inside of me.

You will never know the truth and the truth will never find you unless you sit yourself down with a good book. Many will run this race but only the persons who endures to the end will win the prize. God has a prize He desires to give to everyone but first we must be baptized in the water and reborn in of the spirit. All have sinned and come short of the glory of God, but runners know that is not were the story ends. Don't ever worry about falling for with Jesus Christ you can get back up with a stronger testimony than before.

Get back into the race and this time you set the pace for the enemy will test your agility, but your faith will defeat them. We see the pretty smile on your face and we know your heart is bigger than any race. This is just one of your many miraculous feats and tell them to stay tuned for greater things we have yet to see. Sow seeds of glory for no one truly knows your story and finish the race with honor because many will honor you. God will catch you whenever you fall and restore your strength one hundred times over whether great or small.

"Did You Dream of Me Pt. 2?"

With only months away, my wife is expecting our first babies. She has been going through numerous test just to make sure that our babies are born healthy. On some days, I feel like I am the one having the babies, because on some mornings, we both are sick. Being the man that I am, I permit her to stay in bed while I press my way to work. The babies are more than a dream come true, they will add more love to our loving family.

The first time we heard the word twins was from her grandmother her granny has a spiritual way of knowing. Our family and friends have called, and they are coming over to help us celebrated the good news. Twins have a way of moving people in miraculous ways and ours are expected to turn heads everywhere. Our home will now take on a new meaning and their lives will be enriched by having the greatest parents. Will they be two boys or two girls? Maybe she will give birth to a boy and a girl, either way we will be happy for them.

Today, when I arrived home my wife was excited, the babies are scheduled to be born around her birthday. I had to calm her down with a glass of warm milk and half of a bag of her favorite chocolate chip cookies. Her birthday is in the middle of the month and twins are slated to arrive around the same time. These little children are transforming our lives and I am just going along for the ride. They are slowly growing inside of her womb and every day she is telling me about her experience.

We planned on having children and to be the best parents that we could be. Money was never going to be an issue with our children, anything we wanted for them is paid well in advance. Why should our children be the least, the last and the lost, especially when these kids have two great parents! I have the financial power to bless our children, and when we desire our neighbor's children will get blessed too! I have dreamt of her and she dreamt of me and now we are dreaming of a wonderful future for our children.

It's a beautiful thing to see her caring for our children and I am the protector, provider and the priest of the family. My job is to sow the seed and to provide for any needs and I am willing to take care of my family. God gave me my wife and then He blessed us with children and I want God to be proud of my every move. I am the first to rise and the last to fall asleep. The last to eat and first to bring groceries into the house to eat. She gets the new car and the kids gets weekly allowances and I am the number one daddy and husband!

My wife had a handsome boy and a beautiful little girl, he looks like his mother and our daughter looks like me. As a man, I am much happier being a father, my kids make me look forward to celebrating Father's Day. Last year my little girl gave me a picture written with crayons. It was of the entire family. Then my little boy built a house out of mud and he was so proud to have made me something. She loves her daddy and my son is closer to his mother. Our prayer is they will be strong adults!

At our annual Family Reunion, we are the most grateful for the many blessings that the Lord has bestowed upon us. We give more because we have plenty to give. We are blessed to be a blessing to others, and our blessings begin with our giving to the family. We are firm believers in giving in accordance to the Word of God. We conduct ourselves as Christians, we honor God, his word and follow his way. We give to live, and we sow to grow and with God our children, children will be blessed. God has blessed us tremendously!!

Having one dream has taken us to places that only God could have orchestrated. Soul mates is what we are, and we did not just find that out. God established that fact years ago. Walking together and praying for one another, helping one another and blessing one another is our desire. When I look into her beautiful eyes I see another world and without her how could I be a complete person? Dream of me whenever you like and love me with all your might, and in the end our God will get the glory!

The secret to our success in this life is prayer, we pray in the spirit and according to the Word of God. Supplications along with much meditation brings about the visitation from the Holy Spirit. God is our supplier of our every need! We cannot live without him! He's the one and only true and living God, and we praise him daily. If you have any need, seek God the lover of your soul. Our dreams become a reality due to our fellowship with Jehovah-God the Father of peace.

We are given a journey through this life and after that comes the judgement. As the head of my family, I find myself sometimes on the bottom when I should be on the top. Being in love with somebody could push you out of your position, but with God we can maintain our strength. She has a mind of her own and I have a mind of my own, but we know God wants us to think and be as one. If we are going higher together, we totally understand our roles as husband and wife, and we will see more blessings from God.

"Direct Deposit!"

Why are you looking for checks to come in the mailbox when God can make a direct deposit?
The God we serve has the ability to instantly deposit things into our spirit and not leave a trace as to how they got there
Each and every day we are the recipients of spiritual deposits but do we praise God for them
What if the air stop blowing and what if the water stops flowing, and if heaven shuts up how would we hear the Spirit?
Because Jesus Christ gave up His life every blood bought believer has total access to heavens best

Every time we open up in the Spirit of Jesus Christ the Lord is more than willing to come in and sup with us
As a believer you have a power that the world cannot find and the only way to use it we have to be clean within
Every person has issues that we cannot fix but by having the Lord on our side we know that help is on the way
In order to speak we all have to take a breath and that is where many Christians miss it they often stop short of a miracle
Failing to open your mouth and voicing outwardly your praise or request will result in an unanswered prayer request

Some people attempt to dance up a storm but only an authentic praise can come from the God who created it
Now that the devil has been cast out of heaven he is moving to and fro trying to mimic what he had before

As God is trying to move inside of you the devil is trying to do the same but God alone deserves our praises

People will fake a dance in the flesh and think they are doing God a favor in the earth

The Lord doesn't need our praise, God has Angels constantly saying Holy, Holy, Holy, to the Lord God Almighty

Why are you trying to make a withdrawal when God did not make a direct deposit into your soul?

You are a thief and a robber, and what is making this so sad is that you are in the house of God

This world sees you and God sees you so why are you acting like a fool when you could have the real thing?

Go to God in prayer and deposit a confession of your sins and wait on the Holy Spirit to overtake your soul from within

It is not okay because you have been taught wrong and God is the righteous way, the truth, and the life

God knows how bad you want to feel His Spirit and He also his ways are not like ours

How could we go forward unless God deposits into our souls the power to get wealth

As soon as you get it the devour comes to take it away but the Lord prayed that your faith would not fail you

The earth is the Lord's and the fullness thereof, and they that dwell therein

Don't become envious because of evil doers but know by faith all of your blessings are being directly deposited.

"Disobedient Children"

Every child is not the same and every child has their own identity but every child is not obedient
They have to learn the ways of the world even if they don't have two parents or a guardian guiding them
Life must go on and they have to learn all they can while they can and that will require some hard questions
If everything we do is easy when would we get to the tough stuff, so we could find out what we are made of
A child is called a child because they are still a child and only after living years on this earth they can be called an adult

Either the child is doing the will of their parents or they are going against the will of their parents
What if God asked you to do something good and you intern desired to do something bad?
Would your actions be overlooked and God just went on about His heavenly duties?
God is not like our parents and God can affect our lives in a far greater manor than our parents
God is keeping a record of everything we think and whatever we do is very much a part of that record

When I were a child I stole pocket change from my parents so I could buy cookies and candy from the store
Sometimes I obeyed them and other times I went against their will but all in all I still was their child

As I became older I discovered the will of God for my life and even then and now I am not totally obedient
The more I learn about my Savior Jesus Christ the more I am not worthy of His goodness and mercy
Every day I thank God for His Son Jesus Christ; because of Jesus I can get back into right standings with God

At no time do we get away with disobeying our earthy father, or our spiritual father, or our Heavenly Father
When God commands us to do something and we take that opportunity to do something else we are wrong
If your Pastor asked you to do something specific and you abuse that opportunity you are disobedient
The Pastor asked you to pray and you took that moment to preach you are a disobedient child
I can only pray that we all learn how to obey their voices and not fall short because of our wayward choices

Every child is reachable and given another chance they could please their earthly and Heavenly Father
With every loving parent they wish all the best for their children and so does your Heavenly Father
Having the love of a father is priceless and knowing the Agape love of God the Father cannot be measured
The Lord has a reward for those who seek His face and you have to bless Him for His amazing grace
We are a thousand times greater by being obedient but we are condemned when we are disobedient.

"Dream"

Early this morning I received a message from God and it was crystal clear to my mind, my heart, and to my soul
I was sound asleep from a long and tiresome day but the God of all creation was passing out visual blessings
I saw myself wearing things that I didn't own and I was doing thing that I have never thought of
I had super human strength and whatever I attempted I succeeded
When I woke up reality became my friend and the dream was something I could not befriend

Either day or night it could happen but the question is what would you do with them
Have you ever dreamed of something that were bigger than your reality?
Soon after you awoke your collective thoughts either confirmed the dream or they quickly denied it?
Your mind will sometimes encourage your desire or it will discourage your intuition
Just as the sun comes up and the moon goes away a dream will come and they will soon pass away

Your intimate thoughts could be the light to a dark situation and the way out of every valley experience
Something within them could become the questions and the answers to this worlds confusion

Every thought comes from God and every dream is God's way of playing a movie within our minds while we are asleep
What God gives to you in a dream may not be for your eyes only but it could be for all the world to see
Some of us are the wheels and others are the steering wheels but we need both of them to call ourselves a functional automobile

Every dream is a gift from God and we should be grateful to have had them to flow through our subconscious
This is why your mind is so valuable and having the ability to think for yourself is priceless
Having the will to fight for a greater tomorrow is called hope and moving in the midst of darkness is called faith
They were not there when your mind was being transformed but they will be there when this entire world is turned upside down
With one dream millions of people could have hope and live a life of progressives

Yesterday, could have rendered dreams that caused you to doubt the will of God for your life?
Tonight, is a good night to dream the impossible dream and pop out of bed with a new lease on life
Tomorrow, it has not come and it would be foolish to put in a premature request for a glorious dream
Say you had a dream and you told that dream to a friend and that friend took your dream and made it a reality?
The moral of this story is to dream while you can and bring them to pass before someone else has the same dream

"Every Stream Leads to the Ocean"

Somebody must step forward and explain the reasons why we are the members of the human race?
Would you teach this generation to embrace the past and search for a greater future?
Could you take the past and bring out the best for the future or are you satisfied with the world as it is?
Should you agree to speak to this situation we are looking for you to take the lead not only in speech but to lead by example
Do your job with tenacity and we will follow and at the end of your life we will honor you for such a great legacy

Either get in the water or stand on the bank and watch the stream continue to flow closer your destiny
Some fish swim upstream and others swim around a lake but the fish with big dreams swim until they get to the ocean
Water is the vehicle that leads us to opportunity but if we are unsure as to who we are we could miss it
Your dream should encourage you to strive to become bigger and better than any other fish in the sea
A lake has a purpose and a creek has a right to exist but only those with vision and dreams can survive in the ocean

Everybody has a gift and or a talent; and what we do with them will affect the entire world

The next generation is counting on us to make it to the ocean and sow our seeds so they could expect an harvest

Why sow your seeds on stony ground when God has made provision for the body of Christ to prosper

Someone or something is desiring to use you for their glory but it is up to you to surrender your will totally

One part of you wants to live a glorious life but first you have to fight through the toils and the strife

Everybody has a purpose in this life whether it is to serve or to be served

The Master has need of you and the adversary desire to sift you as wheat

The heart of the King is in the hands of God and you have the right to worship and praise The Creator God

All you have to do is to try God first and yield to Him and the rest is His story

God can work miracles through the gifts He has given to you and even greater works you shall do

We cannot discount the value of our neighbors because we don't have enough money to buy the block

They have a purpose and you have a purpose and together God can work miracles through all of His children

At some point we have to touch and agree that the Lord will make Himself strong and move mightily in the earth

Look unto the hills from wince comes your help knowing that all of your help comes from the Lord

I know it is scary to see the big ocean but through faith every little stream is the beginning of your ocean experience

"Everything Comes With Instructions"

Everything in this world comes with instructions but it is up to us to follow them step by step
Please show me one thing that you mastered without any instructions?
Who taught you how to breathe; who taught you how to eat; and why it is impossible not to stop?
How could the most intelligent beings on the earth not recognize the most powerful force that alone created it?
Just because I am asking these questions don't mean that I have all of the answers

Always remember the inventor had to painstakingly create their invention and they should know how it works
We all are searching for those correct thoughts to these puzzling questions
Thank God for the Holy Bible because this world would be totally confused without it
How do I know of a place called heaven and why am I not going to hell; because somebody gave me precise instructions
How do I know that I have a spirit that lives in a fleshly body that is sustained by my soul?

If you knew more than the creator, the author, and the inventor then why are you totally uninformed?

Our elders are called elders for a good reason and it would do all of us some good to discover their earthly purpose

What if God chose not to use me to write these profound words and what if we did not have the proper instructions?

God has written His pathways to peace, joy, and love, and now it is up to us to study them and to follow them

There is nothing new under the sun and God knew our purpose before He created the heavens and the earth

All of us had to learn our crafts from someone or by reading the manual that came with the project

I am so glad God did not leave our Salvation in the hands of a man who was formed and shaped in iniquity

You can have this world and all of its vain glory because one day Jesus Christ is coming back with the true meaning of the story

Don't ever think you are the answer to every questions because all of us will die with questions about our souls

God is so good He will give us a warning before He gives the command to allow the fall

You will enjoy these earthly pleasures when you take the time and learn how they actually work

We were born for a reason but if we think we have a better reason as to why we were born then something is wrong

This earth is only temporary but our souls will live forever and that is why God sent His only begotten Son Jesus Christ to save us

We all can live our lives to the fullest and serve the Savior at the same time; and still live with Jesus for eternity

Jesus said "Take My yoke upon you and learn of Me for My yoke is easy and My burdens are light"

"Fear Is Never Bigger Than My Faith"

If fear is the evidence of not having faith then faith is the evidence that fear is not within our members
If a seed has to fall to the ground and die before it could bring forth a bountiful harvest what about us?
At first it is so hard to believe and only God knows our measure of mustard seed faith
The life that we are living is worth nothing without faith because with faith we could believe for greater
Why have fear when you could believe and how could you have faith without God inside of your heart?

Whatever we edify the most will become greater than anything we could ever think or imagine
Have you ever faced a situation that you thought was bigger than the highest mountain?
Have you ever yielded all of your members unto the Spirit of the Lord and stood on His Word and moved a mountain?
Faith says I can and fear says I cannot and God gave us the choice to choose
Between the two
Do you see yourself fulfilling all of your achievements by faith or do you fear the uncertainty of the next moments?

Why have a measure of faith and not use it to grow higher than any earthly situation

Those test and trials are for more than crying over they are designed by God to get you to the next level

The trying of your faith works a greater level of patents and with more patents we could continue to use our faith

The faith we have was not free; as a matter of fact Jesus Christ Himself used His faith while hanging on the cross

Faith is the greatest tool to use whenever we are faced with any situation that our hearts could not feel

God did not give us the spirit of fear but of love, joy and a sound mind

I cannot take my faith and give it to you but I can take my faith and help you overcome your fears

We can touch and agree for a greater level of faith that will only render us a greater level of victory

God so loved the world He gave His only Son and because Jesus Christ used His faith we can use ours each day

When we have been converted in the faith we are to go back and strengthen our brother

With faith I can speak those things as though they where and by having faith in God I have the power to wait on Him

Nothing can move unless the Lord gives it motion He also gave us the power to move things by using our faith

Our faith is of God the Father and fear is of the father of lies the devil; now who is your daddy?

I believe God over anything and with a measure of faith we all have the victory over death, hell, and the grave

Fear will try your faith but faith in God cast out all fear

"Fifty Years Later!"

How could you speak of something that you have never lived and boasting on subjects that are far beyond your understanding
Time has a way of teaching lessons that education could only record the history as it is lived
Come and go with me down the road called history and relive the way life used to be
We had no choice in the matter because our elders formed and shaped us into honorable adults
I can take all that you know and put it the top of an ink pen and still have room for one more sentences

Please don't think you know more than me when in fact I am the reason why you are in this world
I can hear your mouth moving but I don't understand what you are saying
Whoever placed you on that pedestal has done you a disservice because a lesson learned is a lesson learned
What you don't know will hurt you and what you do learn in the process will save you in the end

If God desire to take you through the valley then through the valley you will go
If God desires to place you on top of the mountain then there is nothing nobody could do stop you
If you feel that your life is not going according to your plans then you could ask the Lord to change them

If you would have asked the Lord before you started then God would have been obligated to bless your life
If you don't get all that you desire in this world then everything you desire and more is stored up high in the heavens

I always said "If I don't get it by fifty then I will not worry about it" but God has the final say
How could I determine how much I could bear and tell God when, what, and how to bless me
When I was young I did some things and said some things that had nothing to do with Jesus or the Kingdom of Heaven
Having lived fifty years there are still some lessons I have yet to learn but I can share everything that I do know
It would be a crime to not open up my heart to the world when my elders shared all of their understandings with me

My prayer is for those individuals who got caught up with the affairs of this world, fifty years later God is still able
Sometimes I want to sing but I cannot and there are times I desire to laugh and I could not find anything funny
I have more time behind me than I have in front of me and I am not worried about dying
Jesus said "My later days will be greater than my former days" and because he said it I am going to believe it
The adversary is a deceiver and a liar, I could not have stood for fifty years without the blood of Jesus Christ covering me
On this earth this life will end someday but that is when my new life with Jesus Christ will start high up in the heavens!

"Flesh Get Out Of My Way!"

We cannot change it and we cannot shake it, our flesh is the house that we live in until we take our last breath
The only thing that separates God's love for us is the vessel that He created but it will not be there always
Before God formed a man out of clay He caused that man to fall into a deep sleep, then God pulled a rib from his side and made a woman
You were never created to die but when the first Adam failed the second Adam paid the total price for the sins of the world
What the flesh could never do the powerful blood of Jesus Christ put us back into right standings with God the Father

God's desire for us greater than we will ever know so study to show yourself approved Until your soul crosses over the River Jordan keep on pressing your flesh to walk according to the will of the Father
If you learn nothing else you should know where your soul is going to spend eternity
They will never express the expediency of our Lords Salvation because they refuse to acknowledge His Omni presence
Because of Christ Jesus I can have faith but this house of flesh wants me to think it is self sufficient

God has washed away all of your sins but your flesh wants to go back time and time again

My desire is to lift you up but your flesh desired to stay down on the ground

My love for you is always and forever but your flesh wanted a part time lover

I wanted to set your feet on a solid rock but your flesh love walking on sinking sand

It is the Lord who supplies all of our needs but our flesh wants us to believe a lie instead of the truth

In this life you have already fallen but living in Jesus Christ His grace abounds that much more

In this moment I desire to run with the wind but my flesh has an issue that my mind cannot comprehend

On some days my mind is willing but this fragile house of flesh has a will of its own

Tell me what tomorrow will bring and I have to tell you to wait and see if we will be a part of it

Deep inside of my mind I can leap tall buildings but the problem comes when my flesh brings me back into reality

The Great I Am is stronger than superman, Jesus can stop the world from spinning with only a thought

Jesus Christ has taken trillions of black hearts and turned them into hearts of flesh

When this house of flesh finally stops working the Lord promised to carry me into my new home in heaven

Today I feel okay but tomorrow I may not, but if I keep the faith in Jesus Christ my eternal fate is never in doubt

We did not ask to be born but sense we are living let us live to live the rest of eternity with our Lord Jesus Christ

"Forced to Grow Up!"

Having nothing materialistic to call my own but I do have my health and strength, and my right mind. Education I do have some and finding a job is necessary for my survival. What I would give to sleep in my parent's home and wake up in the morning with a hot breakfast on the table. Children are children because they are birthed into this world and at some point, a child must grow up into a young adult. We all know a child has nothing to offer but themselves because they are immature beings and our hearts go out to them.

I surely could use a nice car and a home to lay my sleepy head safely before I close my eyes. I don't make enough money to live a bountiful lifestyle with my numerous roommates we can have a decent place to live. I thank God for my mom, for my cell phone is on a family plan and this is a necessity without the total expense. I have so much to do as a young adult for when I lived at home my parents assisted me in everything I did. Have you noticed the last four sentences started with "I", because I am now forced to grow up and be on my own!

My immature thoughts are all I have and with them I desire to support myself and build a prosperous future. I'm determined to feel the total experience and if I fall I promised my parents that I would get back up. Having a church life is very important for my survival and with God on my side, I think I'm going to be alright. Me against the world and me against myself, and whenever things get hard I say thoughtful prayers to my God. Where would I be without God for with my God I have hope, I have faith, I have trust, and all and all my God provides for me.

There is so much I don't know about establishing a wholesome lifestyle, keeping my freedom, and staying safe. I am growing up the right way and my support team is always there when I need some advice and some financial support. The light bill is mine, the water bill is mine, the gas bill is mine, the cable bill is mine, and the grocery bill is also mine. Whatever happened to having all the fun? Will those days ever come back into my life before I get 100? Day in and day out the time keep rolling on by and I must keep pace with the test, the trials and unforeseen situations.

Economical, opportunities are afforded to those who prepare themselves for an unpredictable workforce environment. Work first and then rest, sacrifice now and celebrate later, save today and live on your budget. Cry now and laugh later you are young, but you will get older. The sooner you plan for your retirement the better it will be. What profits a man to gain the world and lose his soul, don't save the world and forget to save yourself? You will be okay focus on what you desire to become and how great of a legacy you want to leave in the earth.

"Four Minus One Pt. 2"

God knows and God cares about His children and if we can trust Him our lives will never be the same
On the day we were married our lives changed forever and who knew controlled substances would play a intricate part
We never put up a wall against foreign objects but they have done the most damage
If I ever wanted to give somebody the praise I have to give God all the praise for saving our marriage
I wanted to say more than the bad stuff and tell the world that God can do way more than I have mentioned

Jesus Christ, is the ruler of my life and I want the entire world to know it
My faith in my God is even greater than it were before because the Lord has brought my family through the storm
I had to keep the faith and hold on for dear life but I never lost all hope in my Lord
My husband had a greater situation than I and if he perished me and the kids would be fine
We slept indoors and had adequate shelter over our heads, and plenty of food to eat each day

The kids never felt the full impact of their father being gone but I felt the pain of him not being there every night
I would wrap myself up in plenty of blankets and cry my eyes bloodshot red until I fell fast asleep

Those moments hurt me like a bad dream that would not go away because I lived it each and every day

Thank God we are over that trial and I pray that we never have to go down that road again

On some days I would welcome any other test other than the one me and my husband where in

Now we have to go to marital counseling because of those things that really affected our marriage

Most marriages fail because of issues that neither partner saw coming and they were not ready for the test

Not that we were so strong but it was the will of God to keep us because we continued to pray

Our faith in God played a major role in the stability of our marriage and today we are happier because of it

Each night we say a word of prayer together and we pray again before we separate for the day

Have you noticed that we have God in all that we do and when asked we would not have it any different

Every marriage needs a spiritual glue to hold it together when this life tries to pull our marriage apart

As a matter of fact we are praying for your marriage and that nothing will separate you and your soul mate

Marriage is fun to experience with someone you love and marriage is a test of one's love for another person

The world has read everything we were going through and they felt our pain because of my husband's addictions

Now that the head of our home is back in place I am going to allow him to plead his case

Hello everyone, this situation could happen to any couple and we really desire to let the entire world know

Please be careful at any holiday celebration because that is when we do not expect to meet the devil

I had a bit of this and a pinch of that and a sip of this and all hell broke loose when I started drinking mixed drinks

The Spirit of the Lord was telling me to stop but my stubborn flesh was encouraging me to drink up

One thing led to another and I was so drunk I threw up on their sofa

My wife was so mad she left me at the party and you know when you are drunk everybody want to be your friend

Me and the boys left that party and went to another social event across town and that is when things got wild

At every party there is going to be plenty women and where there is single women there is going to be trouble

I had not been out in years and I vowed to myself to never smoke again but on that night I did what the Romans were doing

When I finally came to myself I was sleeping with somebody else, I wanted to leave but they started smoking again

One thing led to another and here I am testifying of how the Lord kept me while I was in the middle of my storm

I knew I had a wonderful family but those drugs sedated me from feeling the pain from neglecting my family

Seems like the more I cried the worse my ordeal became and pretty soon I had lost all hope in myself

I thank God for a praying mother and I truly praise God for my praying wife

The rest of this story I might not be able to finish because the Spirit of the Lord was my protector

My wife thought I was shooting up and smoking marijuana when in fact this situation was worse than that
My feet were swollen because I stood up all the time and my hands were black from digging through the trash
What I was hooked on something I care not to disclose and I thank God that I didn't take off all of my cloths
I thought my past was behind me but when I dropped my guard that is when the devil found me
Please keep us in your prayers and we will do the same, the devil is out to destroy everybody who loves Jesus
God did not say they would not try but no weapon formed against a child of God will never prosper

I feel more confident in my walk with God now that I have been tested and that storm only made me better
Like Job I went through my test and today I have the scars to prove that I came out with double for my trouble
I am a blessed man with a blessed wife, we have three children a dog and a cat, and Jesus Christ as our guiding light.

"Fresh Flowers"

Could I give you something that is near and dear to my heart and I pray that you receive them in the same light
You have blessed me in so many ways and now it is my time to repay every last one of your favors
Please say yes to my graciousness and never say no to something I truly want to do for you
Open up your mind and receive these gifts of love and open up your heart to my gentle touch
You have never harmed me and you always had my back when I were going through my test or trials

God grew them just for you and I picked them just for you and this beautiful moment is all yours
I hope I have done your heart well because I took my time and picked out each flower with love
Roses are red, violets are blue, God gave me a simple message and that is "I Love You!"
The flowers are just the start to all that I have for you I have bought you several presents to add to your surprise
Putting into words as to how I truly feel is so easy to do, when the person you are writing about is the love of your life

No other person is worthy of this honor because they have not been here to protect my fragile heart
We are here to pray together as we continue to grow stronger and I am so happy to be madly in love with you

I enjoy when we block out a weekend for ourselves and celebrate the union that God has joined together

Our relationship is greater than the word we are rewriting the definitions and adding in the statement "Two hearts beating as one!"

Every sense we met I have been your object of desire and you are the person who set my emotions on fire

I appreciated your first kind words, every time you come into my presence I am still grateful to have you in my life

If I start to cry you are the only person who would understand, who I am and where I came from

They hurt me after I gave them my heart but you held me close and have never let me go

My prayer today is for our marriage to always stay as one, until God calls one of us home

Stay as sweet as you are and please don't try anything new because everything you have done is wonderful

Fresh are your kind words and living with you is like taking a breath of fresh air

My days are worth more than life and my nights are peaceful and quiet

God have ordained our love from above and heaven has stamped it with smiles and laughter

You have done all that you could to make mine and your life a beautiful event

These moments are not outside of our character and we want only the best for our lives together.

"Fruitless Vessels!"

With all seriousness no man cannot live a bountiful life without fruit and he will not have edible fruit unless he is rooted
The deeper the root the sweeter the fruit and the greener the leaf the healthier the tree
Now we can see why some people are not bearing fruit because they are not rooted to the source of life
It would be nice to go where I want and to do all that I want to do but if I want to live I have to stay rooted
Walking at this level in Christ Jesus takes some time and a babe in Christ has to wait on God for spiritual maturity

Some fruits are good and others are bad but this does not apply to a fruitless person
The person without a dream or a vision is a person without hope and a hopeless person cannot bear fruit
How could we live each day and not have fruit from our labor and the joy of the Lord inside of our hearts
Teach a man how to read and he can read any book but when you read to him the words are not as important
Who you are cannot be measured but if there is no fruit then the evidence is obvious

Every tree that God plants will yield a harvest and that harvest will be plentiful for this and the next generation
Sinners and Saints alike could come to the cross and eat the bread from heaven and be saved

The mercy of God reigns on the just and the unjust this is why we cannot judge a tree by the fruit it brings
In those seasons of plenty all of the nations of the world will sing and shout over the bountiful harvest
When the elders pray and the ministers minister the body of Christ is guaranteed the victory

The vessel that turns away from sin and turns towards the Word of God may grow weary but they will not fail
What is that hanging from your tree is it real fruit or is it plastic fruit that looks like the real thing
The elders know the way and they know it takes time in the Word of God to grow strong spiritually
God can use anybody as a vessel for the Kingdom but the vessel has to wait until their fruit is ready for harvest
Eating green fruit will make you sick and moving without the Spirit of God is never advised

The fruits of the Spirit is love, joy, peace, long suffering, temperance, meekness and faith
This is a very serious subject and many are attempting to help the body of Christ without knowing Jesus Christ
Walking over people may work out in the world but that mentality will cause you to be judged by God
I know you mean well and Jesus knows it to but your actions are not according to the will of God the Father
Slow down my sister and please be more patient my brother one of these days we all are going to heaven together.

"Give God Something to Work With"

Why pray and not move and why make a move without stating your purpose in prayer?

I too want the world and all of its benefits but unless I act according to the will of God then I am out of order

Unless a seed falls to the ground and dies it cannot bring forth a great harvest

Seek yea first the Kingdom of heaven and all of His righteousness and all of these thing shall be added unto you

All of the promises of God are rooted in purpose and if God did not have a purpose then He would not have made a promise

You can have all that you desire in this life because God said you could

Even the sinners think they are going to a better place but the only problem is they don't know how to get there

Jesus Christ is the way the truth and the life now what is your next move

The way has already been made but if you don't know it then how could you possibly benefit from those promises

If you were homeless you would seek shelter but if you were spiritually homeless would you try to find God?

When Moses stood at the edge of the Red Sea and the enemy were fast approaching God commanded him to stretch out his rod
When Job had lost everything including his family he waited patiently on God to turn his situation around
When the woman was at the well she did not realize who Jesus was until He told her all about herself
When I needed a healing I placed all of my faith in Jesus Christ and the Lord moved on my behalf and healed me
Whenever you need something from the Lord Jesus Christ just act in faith and believe and never doubt His power

There is an anointed power available for you whenever you call those things as though they where
What would you give to the Lord in order to encourage Him to move on your behalf?
People will always require from you the end result because they are doubtful about their own faith
God will never ask for something that you don't have but He does desire to have your whole heart
The only way to God's heart is by faith and when you use your measure of faith every window in heaven will open

I want you to have everything you desire from the Lord but like I said before you have to do your part
Have you studied the Word of God with an open heart and allowed Jesus Christ to overwhelm you with heavenly desires
The only thing holding up heaven is Y-O-U, Jesus Christ was ready to bless you before you were born
Generations have past and yet and still the everlasting power of our Lord is dwelling here on the earth.

"Give Honor Where Honor Is Due"

Are you worthy to receive the honor that only scalars and mighty men are worthy to receive?

Are you positioning yourself to serve now and to be given a starry crown later?

Are you always the last person to comprehend whatever is being taught?

Are you willing to do whatever it takes to be honored in these last and evil days?

Honor will only come to those who are worthy but some people are willing to steal, kill, and to destroy to get it

What have you done to deserve such a great honor and if it is possible could you please tell the world

Usually the people who are at the top have already made a valid contribution to the human race

Where are your books and where are your prodigy's and what generations are profiting off of your wisdom?

To be honored is a serious event and it is to never be taken for granted

If you are not sitting at the head of the table then it must not be your time to be honored

Someday there will be a discovery for cancer and then the entire world would be cancer free

Who were the person that created the method to harness electricity?

Who discovered the process of splitting an Atom?

Name for me the man who successfully had the first open heart transplant?

We had no idea that was you who brought change to our situation and made our hearts glade again?

Some of us are so smart that we don't need nobody to assist us in doing anything

When did one person become so intelligent and became an Island unto themselves?

There were people walking on this earth way before we got here and I recollect it will be people here after we are gone

How many chickens have you raised but nobody can beat you eating chicken?

Something is wrong when the next generation refuses to honor the previous generations contributions to this society

God created us to work together no mater our creed or color

One man plants the seed and another man cuts the tree; then another man supplies the hammer and another man brings the nails

One woman cooks and another woman eats; one woman prepares the wound while another woman performs the surgery

One man calls the plays and another plays the game; one man is called the boss while another man performs the work

One woman and one man comes together as one and within nine months the human race is extended to another generation

"Go Hard or Go Home!"

Bring only your best for this could be your last chance to rise above the rest. They came to display their best and to show you why a prepared person is far greater than a rookie. Your attitude must be of a certain level before you step onto the field or you will be intimidated, pressured, and tempted to give up. Work on your game because it is all you have and when you show up don't forget to bring it with you. Scream if you need to, jump if you need to, bounce if you need to, run, if you need to, do what you need to do!

Wake up! For what's in front of you will command your undivided attention and if you are not ready it will break you into little bitty pieces. The strongest part of you is your mind not your body, the weakest part of you is not having a plan of action. Come on "Champ" this is the day, this is the hour, this is the moment, this is your time to shine, this is the time to claim the championship. Remember to "Go Hard or Go Home!", without a belt, without the trophy, without a ring, without the pennant, without the game ball, and without popping bottles of champagne. Winners have all the fun while losers simply go home.

Picture yourself on a poster hanging on a kid's wall, and the youngster is mimicking your actions. Five, four, three, two, one, swish, touchdown, goal, count it, you made it! That is a wonderful feeling and you are responsible for their joyful moments. They have never trained on your level, but they are excited to see you achieve your goals. Turn the light off and go to bed their mother said, all because you won the game and became a national hero. You prepared yourself for the fight of your lifetime and did what your mother said to do "Knock them out!" Mothers have an ability to inspire a child and mothers are never happy to see their child lose a battle.

Heroes are made of zeros and winners are made of losers, in a race between thousands only one person will win. Are you prepared to suffer through your own adversities to be remembered as the greatest to stand on the stage? Are you willing to feel the pains of extra innings, overtime, second serves, more time on the clock, or come back tomorrow? Winners are tough, winners are ready for anything, winners are not cowards, winners are not chickens, winners are winners because winners always win.

Challenges are designed to make you or break your will to compete. You cannot afford to let them see your weaknesses or they will pounce upon them and defeat you my friend. Get into a huddle and make up a plan, and when you come out on the floor see them as little ants and yourself as the giant. Don't underestimate them because of their size for young grasshopper that would be unwise. There is a powerful lion in the hearts of men and they could rise above everything you had planned. "Go Hard or Go Home!"

"God Can Do Even More"

If you think you have seen it all just wait and see God do the impossible
God have made a way out of no way and paid bills that were months past due
The Bible is still true and God will do what He said He would do but without faith we doubt the abilities of our God
The tears you have falling from your eyes could be tears of joy if you tried having faith in God first
Take this moment in time and make up your mind to always seek God first

The more we study His Holy Word the greater our works and the more God could reveal His greatness in the earth
The Word of God is the true and living Word of God and every true believer know this to be a fact
Never again would you wonder why and for the rest of your life God will miraculously bless your entire life
Verse after verse was given by God to transform our lives from total death into total life
Where you are now is really in a confused state because when God opens your eyes you will have total understanding

Because of sin we are consumed but because of the righteousness of Christ we are eternally blessed
This world will never stop and offer you the Salvation of Jesus Christ because they are warring with the body of Christ

Their truth will be counted as filthy rags and the wisdom of our God will last forever

You have traveled thousands of miles just to find these words and now your life will never be the same

No longer would you follow the knowledge of this world because the wisdom of God is what you longed for

God said He would do it when we the children of God yield ourselves unto Him

Deny yourself so you would not fulfill the lust of the flesh; know that sin separates us from God

Membership has its privileges and to be saved the Jesus way gives us access to all of heavens best

God said to take His yoke upon us and learn of Him and what comes next is never seen but by faith we can see them clearly

All that we desire in heaven and earth is on the tips of our tongues but the greatest gift from God is Jesus Christ His Only Begotten Son

Ephesians 3:20 KJV

God is able to do exceedingly abundantly above all that we ask or think according to the power that worketh in us.

1John 3:23 KJV

And that is His commandment that we should believe on the name of His Son Jesus Christ and love one another as He gave us commandment.

Proverbs 8:19 KJV

My fruit is better than gold, yea than fine gold; and my revenue than choice silver.

Matthew 6:30 KJV

Wherefore; if God so clothe the grass of the field; which today is and tomorrow is cast into the oven, shall He not much more clothe you, O ye of little faith?

"Heavenly Rest"

As I lay my head on a pillow and close my eyes the world around me will never stop me from sleeping
I may not sleep for eight hours but in the morning I will feel refreshed
The peace of God will free my thoughts and the rest for my soul will be outstanding
I am tired for following this world of sin but I will rest because my God controls the soul that is within me
My faith in the Lord Jesus Christ pushes me to live right, and to put my hands to the plow and never look back

I will rest in the Spirit of the Lord and the peace of God will surpass my own understanding
Everyday this old feeble body grows closer to the grave and my soul reaches for Jesus Christ the Anointed one
I gladly embrace the test and I willingly press through my trials, for on the other side is heavenly rest
This old world cannot hurt me for my weary soul they cannot see but the trials I had to face, my God has sustained me

No one can destroy what they cannot see and they cannot hinder the heavenly rest the Lord has prepared for me
Falling asleep could be trying at times but resting in the Lord is so sweet it frees my natural mind
My thoughts are righteous and my mind is stable because each day our Lord is able to regulate my heart

My thoughts come from God and I display him in my conversations with others. I was taught to treat people the way I desire to be treated.
I desire to do unto others as they would not do unto me and to bless those who desire to be blessed

As I rest tonight I pray that the Lord gives me dreams and visions of resting safely in His powerful arms
My body will be rested because my spirit is connected to a God who loves and cares for me
Only the enemy would make up noises when a child of God desires to rest from having a weary day
If it is not somebody's big mouth it is their loud car pipes that could cause a moment of unrest
I stretch forth my hands and speak words of faith and the Spirit of the Lord changes the atmosphere

Now I can rest because the power of God is working in my favor and the enemy has no clue as to what just happen
Rest my feeble body and be at peace my weary soul because my spirit is in the hands of my Lord
I prayed for heavenly rest and the Holy Spirit came in and blessed my soul with peace from glory
An Angelic host surrounded my entire family and because I prayed for rest they brought peace to the entire world
With all of my heart I prayed by faith and with all of my soul I let the Lord have full control over my situation
I trust in the Lord God and I believe in the blood of Jesus Christ and the rest is life everlasting.

"Ho, Ho, Ho!"

Some of you may think this poem is about Santa Claus, when in fact it is really about our Lord Jesus Christ
This is being written in order to open the eyes of the blind and to present the truth of God the Father
Once a year the world gets excited about one certain date when in fact that particular date is not the birth of Jesus Christ
If I had my way I would speak truth to this matter and tell this world they are not celebrating the truth about Christmas

It is okay to pick out one date in particular and to make it Holy unto the Lord
The only problem I have with this event the focus has been twisted from the birth of Jesus to the coming of Santa Claus
When the world says Ho, Ho, Ho, it is a direct insult on the status of our Lord and Savior for He is Holy, Holy, Holy.
The Savior is a male image of the redemption of mankind and even that has been mimicked by Santa Claus

Santa Claus is coming down from the north pole and Jesus Christ is soon to come down from heaven above
Santa's rein deer represents the clouds and his elves represent the Angels of God
The presents represents the reward that Santa will have with him and Jesus will also have a reward with his coming
Why is it that Santa Claus will come on the same day as the birth of Jesus Christ?

The devil has picked the perfect date it is on the same day of our celebration just to deceive the entire world
People who operate in the flesh spend their money and those who are in the Spirit bow down and worship the Savior
We praise the Lord for who He is, not for the material things this world can give
Does your Christmas experience consist of things or does it move far beyond this worlds empty dreams?
You can buy anything to make Christmas joyous but when it comes to your soul only Jesus
Christ can save you

Year after year we think we are celebrating the Savior when in fact we are grieving the Holy Spirit
Generation after generation are failing to uphold the glory of Jesus birth and the world is suffering because of it
The real meaning of Christmas is celebrated all year long and when you need something special from God just pray
The carnal person say happy holidays but the redeemed of God always say Merry Christmas

Some have even tried to take Christ out of Christmas by making up a term called Xmas
There are some who enjoy having one foot in sin and the other in the world
True Christians love the Lord all year long and at any given time they could break out in a Christmas song
God is giving us time to accept his Son and to stop playing rein deer games with ourselves and calling it celebrating Jesus Christ.

"How Long Not Long"

If God says something would not take long then it does not matter how long it takes
The start and the finish of anything begins with God and the completion of anything is His handy work
My child don't worry about a thing nothing is going to happen until I the Lord gives the command
I will come back sooner than you think and I have my reward with Me
Keep your lamps trimmed and burning for no man knows the day or the hour of My second coming

What if a man opens his mouth and speaks boldly will God invoke His power and shut that mans mouth?
Every man has a right to open their mouth and speak but every word a man says will meet him at his judgment
Life and death is in the power of the tongue and with it we can speak those things into existence
If it is taking forever to receive from the Lord then you need to check what words have you spoken out of your mouth
Chose your words wisely and speak them quit expeditiously and trust in the Lord to bring them to pass

Is a generation too long to wait for a change and if it does not happen right now it may never happen?
Your generation could be the generation that finally work while it is day

Cursed is the man who puts their hands to the plow and looks back at wince they came

Down through the years many prayers have been said by the righteous and now harvest time has come

Thank all of your elders for staying on the wall and for being obedient to the Word of God

Could we make time speed up or slow down and predict the movements of the heavens and the earth?

Search the scriptures for the answers and once you find them allow the Spirit of the Lord to settle them in your heart

Witches and warlocks think they know the truth but in the end their predictions are counted as sin

Remember there is an adversary who desires to stop you from serving the everlasting God our Father

Keep your hearts and minds stayed on the Lord and the Lord will cover you with His precious blood

May the times we have spent together be fruitful and progressive with today as an example of the signs to come

Whenever the moment is quiet and still that is when we are looking for great things to come from our God

Where you are right now did not take a lifetime and that single fact should settle your mind

Always be ready to give your all because we never know how long we have left on the face of this earth

The Saints of God never worry about the signs of the times because we know who holds today, tomorrow, and the future.

"How So Easily Offended?"

You must know the power that is inside of you is greater than anything on this earth
Never should a person of your rich character become moved by the ignorance of others
They have the right to act as they please because they are made of flesh and blood just like us
You have to continue to grow along with uncertainties and accept the positive and reject the negative
Be strong in the Lord and in the power of His might and use the criticism of others as your stepping stones

Where is your thick skin and where is your mustard seed of faith, never again will you be so easily offended
Just because an issue arises doesn't mean it has a permanent place in your life
Our emotions are extensions of our inner thoughts and sometimes our emotions are out of place
This life can become difficult when associating with others who think they are far greater than yourself
You have to know that every day is not going to be the same but each day is another opportunity to change

People are going to be people and we have to let them be whom God allow them to become
Could my confusion derive from my interpretations of how others should live and behave
To become bitter over something that you could not possibly control is not being wise over your personal affairs
Every person is not the same and why would anybody think any different
As the Lord opens your heart to the situation you have to learn how and when to close it to minimize your emotions

When are we going to understand that our emotions are connected to our flesh
The flesh has no foundation to depend upon because in the end these earthen vessels are turning back into dust
Knowing the truth about ourselves is more valuable than rubies and more precious than pearls
Our emotions do have their place but they should never push us into a situation that compromises our integrity
Please allow me to reiterate my point, don't get so wrapped up in your own pointless emotions

Look at where you could be if you didn't give space to issues that had no realistic value
People will try to push your buttons just to see how you would react and when you act unseemly then they are happy
For once you should surprise them with an intelligent response and afterwards keep your mouth closed
Make their efforts to break you humanly impossible and as they sow seeds of discord God is reversing the curse
I think you got the message but will you put it into practice and stop acting like an emotional wreck.

"I Am Tired And Homeless!"

If I could have seen this coming I would have been the first
person to have avoided it
They ambushed me and left me for dead and now with this
second leash on life I have to give it my all
I have gone from busting tables to washing dishes and when
people don't know you this life could be even harder
Would you believe that I have several years of college education
to my credit and when I can, I do plan on finishing
First I have to overcome this temporary homeless situation and
get my entire life back on track

Now I know the importance of having relatives that I could call
on because I have fallen into a ditch
They wanted me to have a fixed address but at this time I am
facing a situation that is bigger than my finances
I was working to support myself but I guess I was not making
enough money to satisfy my creditors
I have become lower than dust but how could that be when we
all came from the same dust from this earth
Realistically, I should be dead because I was shot several times
and I have a illness that requires that I eat a balance diet

God has heard my cry because He sent me some help when I could not get my own family to bring me food to eat

All of my prayers were not in vain but they have entered into heaven and God has sent back to earth my answers

All of those nights sleeping on the sidewalk and waking up only to find somebody had stolen all of my stuff

Let me ask you "What would you do if on tomorrow you found yourself without a home to call you own?"

Never did I ever imagine myself in such a predicament but within my heart I know that I am not the only one

I am not a lazy person and I am not a very good beggar, the great person I once knew is still living deep inside of me

I have hope for tomorrow even though everywhere I turn all I can see is sorrow

I would work if somebody gives me the chance and I will continue to pray until God turn this nightmare into happiness

Whenever I think of why, I think again and come up with nothing that makes any good sense

Whenever I think all is not lost, I have to know that God knows that I am living and sleeping under this bridge

God sent me an angel who did not count it robbery to sit down on my soiled blanket and talk to me

At first I thought he was just another homeless person who wanted to talk some sense into my head

He spoke to me on my level and before he left he gave me his card and twenty dollars and directions to his church

As the time quickly went by I asked my other homeless friends did they want to come along and attend church

They gave me a stern look and a convincing response as to their plans for the evening

My change happen so fast as though nothing had ever happened but this time I give God all of the glory

One day I am laying on a blanket and the next day I am living in a four bedroom house with every known amenity
My angels have never mentioned anything about money but they did reaffirm this whole situation with respect
Now I am learning a new trade and I have a wonderful place to live, things are surely changing in my life
They are not putting pressure on me to complete any task but they are showing me what to do as a friend suppose to do
One angel helped me and then another angel carried me away to a beautiful place of rest

I know the devil is looking for me under that bridge but presently I am hid in God according to my Lord and Savior Jesus Christ
Nothing on this earth has the power to pluck me out of his hands my God is my Alpha and Omega
The Word says the devil is moving to and fro seeking whom he my devour and that is not were the story ends
My Lord said he would never leave me nor would he forsake me, and as a matter of fact He has never left me

How could this be when a homeless person like myself never gets a break from humanity who looks down on us
People on the street think homeless people are less than humans when in fact we are the same as everybody else
Every day I prayed for God to bring a change and I purposely fasted because of involuntary starvation
These moments would not be so bad if I did not have a medical problem that requires me to eat every four to six hours

I refuse to become a victim of this tragic situation and be remembered as a homeless person who fell through the cracks

This morning when God touched me with His finger of love I sat up as though I were still sleeping on the cold sidewalk
No longer am I hungry but I am tired from learning a new trade and tonight when I get finish working I will sleep like a baby
No more surprises as to where I would sleep and being awakened by something that crawls throughout the night
Any homeless person could get used to this lifestyle but I know and you know that all good things must come to a end
God is showing me how I should be living and if I seek His face my lifestyle would be even greater than this

My family cannot believe it and my enemies cannot find me because God is hiding me inside of His Holy hands
I am forever grateful to all of my angels for answering the voice of God and for witnessing to a wretch like me
Nobody deserves to sleep under a bridge and beg total strangers for bits of change for food and other things
With this new outlook I am going to give it my all and if God loves me this much I cannot wait to see myself in the future
I pray that you never go through being homeless but I do pray that you find it in your heart to help those who are.

"I Can Always Talk To God"

Anytime of the day or night is just right to talk to my God
God is waiting for me to fall down on my knees and ask whatever
I want, desire, and He knows all that I need
There is no need for me to start begging the Lord for the things
He has already promised
I guess when you have never studied the Word of God and finding
something to talk about could be a little scary
Last night I tried to call you but your voice message encouraged
me not to hang up but to leave a detailed message

Sometimes we laugh out loud and sometimes we sit quietly
listening to each other's thoughts
The Lord knew my thoughts before I could formulate them inside
of my mind
The relationship we have originated up in the heavens and it was
solidified by the miraculous power of His Son Jesus Christ
The joy of the Lord is my strength and when I am weak that is
when my God is strong
Way before anything happens my days are filled with getting to
know more and more about the King of Kings

God's ways are not our ways but in all cases God's ways are the
best ways

When He leads me I have discovered peace and harmony but whenever I take the lead I ended up totally confused
God's instructions are sound and true and His infinite wisdom supersedes anything my mind could ever conjure up
I did not hear the voice of God the first time He spoke but my spiritual ears have developed through the Word of God
Today we had another conversation and the more my Lord talked the greater my life became

Whenever you refuse to answer my calls and place your phone on permanent voice mail is no longer a worry
Even if I don't hear from my God I can trust the contents of our last conversation
Whenever I truly want to hear the voice of God all I have to do is to steal away with a copy of His Holy Word the Bible
Moments like those are better than anything in this world because heaven is speaking into my soul
Have you ever wondered why I never call and even without your input I am growing physically, mentally, and spiritually?

Hello Lord, are You too busy to talk or would You desire that I use my faith to affirm Your love for one more moment?
Have I told You that I could not make it without Your voice speaking life, love, and peace over my life
One of these precious moments I am going to shut my eyes and open them up in the bosom of Your love
Then I will see You face to face and sing Holy, Holy, Holy to the God of all creation
Thank You Lord for calling me blessed and thank You Lord for making a way; and I thank You for calling out my name

"I Don't Feel A Thing"

What is all of the dancing and shouting about because right
now I don't feel a thing
Whatever has gotten into them is making them act like fools and
I choose to keep my dignity
I can stand on the sidelines of life and still possess many cars,
houses, land, and a pocket full of cash
While they dance and shout I am going to work and save my
money, and whenever I need something I can buy it
They beg God for things and bow down to a God that they cannot
see, I have a sure thing called cash money and good credit

I asked God for something in particular and to this very day I
have not gotten it nor have I heard from heaven
As a matter of fact they make me sick how could they shout when
God have not brought them out of their situation
I will shout when God brings me out and until then I am staying
quiet and sitting still in my seat
Numb is the word that comes into my mind and the way I see it
I will have this characteristic for the rest of my life
What do they feel that takes them out of themselves and carries
them into a spiritual state?

They keep on shouting hallelujah and glory to God in the highest,
and I have nothing to say out of my mouth
Unless they could meticulously explain to me how they do this
strange act my emotions will remain intact

Why should I let go when I don't know where I am going and more importantly when am I coming back
Now they want my money for something they called miraculous ministries
This is going to be the last time I accept an invitation to come to anybody's church services

I just pray that nothing happens within my lifetime and cause me to ask God for help
When I go to the club they have the music so loud I cannot hear myself think and soon after I am encouraged to drink
I guess the DJ wants me to feel the spirit and shuffle my feet to the sound of the beat
If I desire I could dance with a woman or a man and if I am mad I will dance all by myself
This is the lifestyle I chose to live and they never ask me to give your God the glory

If your God is so powerful then why is my life so jacked up and I have become accustomed to living in bondage?
Did you pray for my total transition or do you continue to pray for money, houses, and material things
Where is the hope for my sin sick soul and could you be the saint to inspire me to surrender all
Could God take my black heart and dip it in His red blood and make all of my sins white as snow?
I want to feel the Spirit of the Lord moving deep inside of me because I gave Jesus Christ my soul to save.

"*I Have Been To Church*"

For all of my life I have wondered what the church has to do with my life.

I see people coming and going with some of them being all dressed up and others are just dressed

Many parishioners throughout my community are honored for what they do out in the public and at their church

One of the faithful members placed in my hand a Spiritual track and that piece of paper surely spoke to my life

With that single track God must have erected a hedge around my soul and propelled me to go inside of the church

If God is real could He come down from heaven and speak to my heart and allow His Holy Spirit to overflow?

The preacher said God could do anything and for the rest of my life I am going to hold God to every word

As a matter of fact I have a pressing need right now and here is God's chance to show Himself strong

Years have gone by and the Lord has been there to cover me and now I will get the opportunity to praise His name

I have met a friend who is closer than a brother but in reality Jesus Christ is the greatest friend I have ever met

The Word of God spoke to my soul and caused my heart to feel His eternal presence

Through my ears I heard from God and through my senses I felt the Spirit of the Lord; while Jesus saved my soul

The world had taken away my attention and for the Spirit of the Lord to save me it took a miracle

They never told me that I was already blessed because they wanted me to deny the existence of Jesus Christ

Now I have a new look on this life and it is to the credit of the Spirit of Jesus Christ

The more I called on God the more He spoke, the more I trusted in Him the greater His Holy Spirit moved in my soul

Man shall not live by bread alone but by every Word that proceeds out of the mouth of God

The Word of God informed me that out of my own mouth I could speak death or life over my own situation

My spiritual man was suffering from not having a edifice to call home and for not having the word deep inside of my soul

Today I thank God for those Saints of old who stood on the wall and continued to pray for my soul

I want the world to know I have been to church and if they could swallow their pride God will save their souls

The church is a institution that was established upon a rock and the gates of hell shall not prevail against it

If you are not aware the church was established for the fellowship of the body of Jesus Christ

There is a Spiritual war going on and it is over the fate of your soul

"I Have Need of Your Seed"

There is something deep inside of you that the world desires to use but I have a greater need of your seed
Tonight before you fall asleep pray that your faith does not fail before I the Lord has the chance to use you
The world has no place to rest your soul but I have gone away to prepare a glorious place as your resting place
Where I am there you shall be also but first I need your voice and the labor of your hands
If you say a simple yes your children, children would never hunger or thirst in the land that they shall inhabit

Unless a seed falls to the ground and dies it cannot have an abundant harvest
You have been chosen to carry out the task that the previous generations failed to fulfill
This time you will not doubt the power of Jesus Christ; that is moving and working deep within your soul
Everywhere your hands touch will become yours and everywhere your footsteps land will become hallowed ground
I Am is the Lord of all flesh and whatever I say will, shall, and My Words must come to pass

I the Lord have been trying for several generations to dwell inside of a totally yielded vessel

I used My Son to redeem all mankind; now broad is the way to destruction and narrow is the way to righteousness

I have searched your heart and soul and your heart of flesh is more than ready to bring your generation into the light

I will move whenever you call and I will supply all of your needs even before you ask

This is My desire and this is My will for your life; and because of your obedience generations will be saved

A person may plant the seed and another may water it but it is the Lord who gives them life

We have life and we have it more abundantly because of the undeserved grace and mercy of Jesus Christ

The Lord is so Spiritually smooth He seamlessly moves in our lives without a trace

The Lord has done trillions surgeries without a physical doctor ever being present and without any anesthesia

The seeds we have inside of our body have been placed there by the creator God who made all of this possible

Will you become the voice for your generation and bring them out of bondage and guide them into the promised land?

Many have fallen into the ditch and I could use you to speak My Words over them to encourage their faith

I give seed to the sower and bread to the hungry nothing has a chance to live unless I the Lord gives it life

You are living only by My amazing grace and you are not consume because of My unmerited favor

I could get by without your fleshly input but what fun would that be when heaven and earth could commune together.

"I Hear You but I'm Listening to God"

This is the day that The Lord has made and when you make a day just for me then I will listen to you. We both are living under the grace of God and with this precious gift we must remain cautious of what we do and say. God is the giver of all life and with these moments in time God is hoping that we continue to seek His advice. Some of us are speaking before we have heard from God and we are proclaiming things are totally out of order. Listen twice before you speak and listen for the confirmation of The Spirit before you say amen.

Say whatever The Holy Spirit says and speak those words with power and authority. Just because you say it does not mean they are true because of what you say may not apply to that person. Seasons change, and people change, nothing is constant except change. God takes the time to listen to our hearts and then The Lord speaks life into our spirit and then our strength is renewed. Many of you are just stirring up dust and when the dust settles God had to clean up the mess.

Unless the Spirit of The Lord confirms those words for me I will take them as words spoken into the atmosphere. Words and things are the same but if you did not know this your words are working against yourself. Why say God is love with hatred inside if your heart and why hate when an abundance of Gods

Agape love is available? Love lifted me from thinking I knew it all because hatred had me thinking I were far better than anyone else. We must note the words we receive and cancel out those words that are contrary to the will of God for our lives.

Life and death are in the power of our tongues and at no time are we to kill the spirit of another person. Only the devil comes to steal, kill, and to destroy, so now why did you come into my life? God is not in a hurry to do anything because He has set things in order and He said they were finished. What is your hurry to speak over my life and to get me to do things that I know are not of God? Whenever we act unseeingly it is a clear indication that we are not normal.

This is getting to be too much because The Word of God does not need all that attitude to work. That is your flesh speaking out loud with the hopes of being accepted by us when at the same time you are rejected by God. What's wrong with you just delivering The Word of God and then allowing The Spirit of God to move in the midst? Dose tone make The Word more effective and could our posture move The Lord more expeditiously? Never think that I am not informed by The Spirit of Jesus Christ because He is the author and finished of my faith.

"If God Be for You!"

We have a power that this world will never understand and when this life is over God will reveal all of His glory
They wonder why we bow down on our knees and pray to a Spirit that we cannot see
We have been visited by the Lord of Lords and when He left He did not leave us comfortless
Through our belief and faith in our Lord and Savior Jesus Christ is enough to bring Him from His throne and into our hearts
Now we can take off the "if" and replace it with confidence in a God who cannot fail

Each day we are tried on every hand and tempted even when we are minding our own business
The good that I should do I end up not doing and the evil that I do was never on my schedule of things
Where would we be without the forgiving power of Jesus Christ moving and working for our good and not for our destruction?
In every case we are victorious because of the miraculous blood of Jesus Christ paid it all on a hill called Calvary
You and I can say yes and amen to the will and the way of God because nothing on this earth could stop His will for our lives

We can lift our hands and open our hearts to the miraculous, wondrous, awesome, and beautiful truths of our God
The question is why haven't this world taken advantage of the freely given power of a all encompassing God?

The person you are is only a fraction of the person you could become with the anointed gifts from God

We are not here to compare our treasures with the tangible, materialistic, and temporary things of this world

Many have desired to become famous and others have denied the claim but all of them had to face the judgment of a merciful God

This fight is not between you and your neighbors but it is a battle between the Holiness of God and evil forces

Nothing in heaven or throughout the entire universe has the power to command the hands of God to move

Power cannot be made it has to be given and without the source of life nothing has the power to exist

The person you are is a gift from God and the giver of all life commands a praise from every vessel

Because of sinfulness you could say within yourself that there is no God but if you do you will become a enemy of the Kingdom

God has plainly stated in His Holy Words that we are predestined in order to give us an expected end

If we look close enough and deep enough God the Father, Jesus the Son, and the Holy Ghost are our only true friends

You can look all around the world and you will never find a closer friend than Jesus Christ

The Lords Words have been placed in a book called the Bible and when we study them the real world will open up before us

Now that you know the truth put all of your trust in the one true and living God

"If I Could I Surely Would"

When I think of your possibilities and what you could achieve
I cannot keep my feet on the ground
All I can see is victories ahead of you and at the end of your life
your children's, children will be proud of you
There are no greater times for your generation all because you
stood up for the least, the last, and for the lost
One moment after the next is filled with nothing but unforeseen
successes
If I were still young like you I would use my time wisely and show
God that I was truly grateful

With some dedicated time and some wisdom from God you will
rise above the competition with ease
A book is your closest friend and with plenty of good friends the
entire world will be jealous of you
Whenever you desire to be inspired your friends are sitting on a
shelf waiting to add to your brilliance
You understand that words are your life and unless you have a
collection of them your life is not worth living
If I were still young like you the world would be my stage and the
audience will know without a doubt that I loved them

To be highly intelligent is a gift and knowing how to use it is a talent that has to be learned by everyone

Thinking you know something great is never a problem but thinking you know more than God is a big problem

Show me single words and I will put them in a sentence; and with a book I can speak beautiful words to the world

You could do what I have done and even more but first you have to dedicate yourself to the race that is being run

During my lifetime some days were surely tough and within yours you should not expect all of them to be easy

Anybody could destroy a perfect dream but this world cannot see God's people with infinite knowledge

They don't know what you have been through but you do have the scars to show for your struggle

The true person deep inside of you has not been revealed but with God all things are possible

A moment in the life of the believer is far greater than living a lifetime of sin

If I were still young like yourself I would continue to call on God in the good times as well as the bad

The world will always judge you by the color of your skin and not by the contents of your character

Down here on this earth God sees us as living happily ever and surely when we get to heaven

They will doubt the words you have hid deep inside of your heart because those words belong to God

The day you say yes to God and no to this world the Lord Jesus Christ will come in and change your life forever

If, I were still young like yourself I would think more highly of myself and show love to the people who don't love themselves

"In My Past but Not in The Present"

Some of you may think I am lying and some of you could think my statements are the farthest from the truth
All I ask is that you would give me the chance to tell the world my story
Please don't try to shut me up before I get started and if you could be patent with me I promise not to mention your dirt
This is my struggle with sinfulness and how it has tested my flesh in so many ways
The person you see is a person who has been tested, tried, tempted, and teased but yet I am still standing

My worldly behavior was considered normal by the worlds standards but my God has a higher standard
They never stopped me from killing myself and as a matter of fact they encouraged my sinful behavior
I was drunker than a skunk, higher than a kite, I was past the point of passing out I was at the gates of hell
Good times was my first name and drop it like it hot was, my middle name and don't stop get it, get it, was my last name
That was my past life and I intend on keeping all of those sinful acts far away from my new life with Jesus Christ

The Word of God is my guiding light and the Holy Spirit is my comforter and Jesus Christ is the Savior of my soul
Nothing in this world is greater than the Word of God and until the end of time nothing ever will
Way back then my soul was starving for God but my lifestyle kept me far away from the only God who could save my soul
Sleeping until the middle of the day because I had stayed out until the sun came up were the norm
The Word of God has opened my eyes to the truth and no longer do I live a lie and calling it having a good time

All of my old friends are wondering what has happen to the ring leader of our sinful group
Every since I gave my life to Jesus Christ all of my sins have been forgiven and what was old has now become new
They said I look the same on the outside but the Lord has made a miraculous change on the inside
I was drowning in a sea of sinfulness and the longer I stayed there the closer my soul was to a burning hell
Why go to hell when I don't have to and why live a life of sin when Jesus Christ has given me the victory over sinfulness?

My closets were filled to the capacity with dirty sinful acts and because of my sinful behavior I could not tell the difference
God has a way that we cannot go under and God has a way we cannot go over we must come in at the door
Jesus Christ is the way the truth and the life; and if you are wondering Jesus Christ is the door called Salvation
I have attended church and I never allowed the church of Jesus Christ to get inside of my soul
I hid behind the collar and I hid behind the uniforms; and I hid under the choir rob and from anything that felt like righteousness

Today I am free in Jesus Christ and I am not ashamed to tell the world about it
All of my closets are squeaky clean and free of skeletons looking for my sinful flesh
I am blessed in the city and I am blessed in the field; and I am living my life to live forever with Jesus Christ
If I fall into diverse temptation I know where I could go to get back into right standings with my Jehovah-God
All of us have sinned and have come short of the Glory of God; now who are we to point our sinful fingers?

"In the Hands of Our Elders"

In this life we will find ourselves in some trying situations and only the hands of God could free us

We serve a merciful God who knows the issues of our hearts but every man does not believe in our living God

Everybody starts out as an infant and if God is merciful then we will grow stronger and into adulthood

The strong must bear the infirmities of the weak and that include the very young and every one of our elders

Honor those who have charge over you and at no time are we to disrespect our elders

The Bible clearly states to call on the elders whenever we the children of God have any simple or pressing issues

The will of God is easy to do whenever we use the Spirit of the Lord to lead us through our storms

God called the young because they are strong and God called the elders because they are wise

Whenever a young vessel tries to get out of line it is the elders job to put them back into their place

From the beginning of time God has not changed the character, the personalities, or the will of all mankind

It is never wise to exclude the powerful hands of God to attempt to bring peace into any confusing situation
Our Lord Jesus Christ is the Mighty God and the Prince of peace
In Jesus Christ will should build our hopes and because of Him we will never be lost
Because of Jesus Christ we now have life and life more abundantly and there are people who still deny His existence
We should proudly display the blood stained banner over our deeply stained sinful hearts

There is only one way to please our God and that is through our mustard seed of faith
Our elders have a great purpose in this life and in the everlasting life that is to come
Why would our gracious Heavenly Father bless us throughout our entire life and forget us when we get old?
When we are out of place we will lose valuable knowledge and without knowledge there will not be an understanding
A child cannot advise an adult and an adult cannot lead an elder but an elder has the wisdom to guide a nation

"In The Middle"

Intro: We were in the middle of living out our dreams, I was in love with him and he was crazy in love with me

Verse #1:
The plans we've had were contingent upon us being together and as we went along they got bigger and bigger
We have given birth to our first child with the plans on having another
He was doing so great on his job and I retired to become a full time mom
Moving progressively through our bills we paid things off in record time
We have a home in the city another in the country and a beach home to call our own

Chorus:
Have you ever been in the middle of putting together a puzzle and someone came along and mixed up the pieces
It feels like the hardest thing to conceive starting over again with one less piece of your puzzle

Verse#2:
I can remember like it happened on yesterday my baby went away to be with God
All the tears I have cried and those days I wish I had died
What a powerful blow to my back it seemed as if I was having a heart attack

Right now my kids are too young to understand and through the years to come they will know their father was a great man
What could I do now to curve their pains but forever we will carry his last name

Chorus:
Have you ever been in the middle of putting together a puzzle and someone came along and mixed up the pieces
It feels like the hardest thing to conceive starting over again with one less piece of your puzzle

Bridge/Vamp:
Today I'm going to lay here and cry until I'm satisfied and on tomorrow I'm starting again
God did it once and I know He can do it again, marriage is a gift between two friends

Out trough:
Our children are still going to college and they will become successful women and men
I believe I'm going to make it through when at his funeral things looked so sad to burry my best friend
I'm over the top and looking forward to things to come with my family living as one

"In The Presence Of Dignitaries"

People sometimes desire to sit in the midst of persons who are the top one hundred movers and shakers
Having the privilege to thrive within their environment is only reserved for those who have passed certain test
Ignorance has no place with intelligence just as stupidity is the opposite end of brilliance
When asked a very important question do you defer the answer to someone else other than yourself?
Have you ever won the approval of your peers or have never elevated yourself in the business community?

What do you think about yourself that would open these doors and ultimately gain you total access?
Are you currently enrolled in any institutions of higher learning?
Have you ever been selected to work as an intern to any high level dignitaries?
Do you know the role you would play if you where voted to represent a ward, district, reservation, or village?
I have all faith in your dreams but a dream is something we are awaiting to see

Empowerment is the ability of a person to gather and having knowledge of something they deem to be valuable
Why spend all of your time learning something that the majority of the world would not except?
Everybody desires to be the first to seek out something that no one has ever done
Whoever said the people you look up to would rise to the top level of leadership and actually become affected?
If you want to sit in the seat of the powerful you have to know what is absolute power

The people you desiring to have as associates are looking to draw the same knowledge from you
When they ask of you your opinions you must instantly give a definitive answer
Who do you think will pay you to know nothing about something?
Words of wisdom are priceless and to have them at your beckoning call is why you went to school in the first place
Give up your free time to study those words that are necessary to gaining access at the Kings table

Are you willing to sacrifice your lifetime for the health and safety of your nation?
The very people you desired as associates have done just that and when you look at their lives it is evident
Please don't be dismayed or discouraged many have desired the same desire and have failed
Think about it this way the world would be in a worse state without prodigies such as yourself
Desire but never beg, want but never plead, seek first the Kingdom of God and the rest will be added unto you

"It's Just My Imagination"

Let me first say thanks for receiving my gift and second I want
to remind you that it is only my imagination
For some people putting words into a particular order is hard
enough but for me it is the gift my God has given
All of the gifts of God are given without repentance and that
should assure the fact that our God is truly Sovereign
I truly hope you are enjoying the ride sometimes sad, but most
the time it is joyful and only God knows how this will end
All of my desires are connected to my heart and my imaginations
are those things I see my God doing in the earth

Have you ever seen yourself doing something that would be
fruitful for your life and believed it to be true?
Because I am connected to the source of life everything I am
thinking came directly from high up in the heavens
I call those things as though they where and I see a greater
future than I could ever imagine
I can even imagine a wonderful change coming over your life and
as you continue to trust in God it will start right now
Whatever I am God made me and whatever I am not is not God's
will for my life

I thought I knew it all but when God ignited my imagination He pushed me into another spiritual rime
Every man has the ability to imagine things but the question is how would he use it
I could have imagined the total opposite but I have chosen to magnify the Spirit of the Lord
They wanted me to write this and make my characters do that and none of it inspired me to answer their calls
With the anointing empowering my desires nothing can get in the way of God getting all of the glory

Sometimes my friends doubt my gifted abilities but without a doubt all of my enemies refused to acknowledge them
My words are my platform and your mind is the stage and together we will enjoy all of my imaginary thoughts
It is hard to hate something you love but each and every day haters manage to hate our imaginary gifts from above
This gift is not exclusively mine but if you ask of God he could fill your request in a short period of time
I asked and God gave them and when you ask God is able to do even greater things for you

I can imagine walking on streets paved with gold and singing Holy, Holy, Holy, to the Lord God Almighty
Up there haters will not make it in and if our God forgives our sins we will never imagine praising His Holy Name again
Our imaginary moments would be over and everything around us will become a heavenly reality
With a belief in God and a confession of my faith in His Son Jesus Christ, I am now living in heavenly places
Living less than one hundred years did not spoil my chance to get back to the place where I originated.

"Judgment Starts at the Church"

I got some good and bad news and both of them applies to every human being

The good news is Jesus Christ has paid the price for all of our sins when He gave His life on Calvary

The bad news is for those persons who are in the house whole of faith and think that they have eternal life

The Word of God plainly states that the judgment of the entire world will start at the church

Even today we can be totally sure of this one fact and never are we to become doubtful about our Salvation

The life that you are living is a blessing and not a curse but that depends upon the God you are serving

Some people love to worship material things but in the end material things have no true meaning

Name me one thing that has the power to save us from our sins and then has the power to give us eternal life?

I pray that you don't live each day like you are your own god but you are yielded and blessed by Jesus Himself

Living in this twenty-first century could be deceiving to some and confusing to others

What things you do will be accounted towards you and those things you don't do just may apply to you
Because you are existing on the this earth should mean more to you than eating, drinking, and having lots of fun
Knowing those facts makes it even more easier to be deceived by the advisory
Some people simply chose to do nothing and take the chance on making into those pearly gates
I know you are smarter than them and you have taken full advantage of the Salvation plan of Jesus Christ our Savior

Work while it is day for when the night time comes no man can work
When your life is over there would be no one standing beside you desiring to pardon your sins
Here's a question "How long has the Lord allowed you to walk on this earth?"
We planted seeds in the spring and harvested then in the summer; and now the fall is almost over and you are not saved?
If you have never said the Salvation prayer Jesus Christ has been waiting over two thousand years to hear your voice

Because you blessed them those acts will be remembered by the God who created the heavens and the earth
Please don't think for a second that this Salvation status is a joke when in fact your soul is in grave danger
If I were you I would fall down on my knees and ask the Lord to save my soul
Please do it while you have the chance because the next moment is not promised to be enjoyable
In short you could already be sitting in heavenly places and not be fearful of bursting hell wide open.

"Just the Two of Us!"

Nothing in this world is stronger than a sibling blood line and I am the oldest of two sisters
I can remember our parents dressing us up as twins when the entire world knew we had years between us
I still have locked away a pair of our baby shoes and the dresses to match we looked so cool
Our mother would do our hair and then dare us to mess it up but leave it to my baby sister she would get us both in so much trouble
I did all I could to keep her from falling and to ensure that we would grow old together as best friends and close sisters

We played childhood games and most of the time I let her win just to keep her from crying
She would cheat and I would turn my head and do like a real sister would do I let her have her way
When we played hopscotch she would touch the line and I never made her go back to the previous number
Her little hands never could beat me in jacks but that never stopped her from trying to gather all ten
Why did we have to grow up and experience the worst of this thing called life

As children our mother purposely created a unbreakable bond between the two of us and it steal stands until this day

If one of us had a piece of candy it had to be broken in half and that was the basis of our training
When one of us got a new dress the other got something similar in size and color
Because we didn't have brothers to share in the household chores we did them all including cutting the grass
On every Christmas we would wrap up a gift and give it to some little kid who had less than we did

I did all I could to cover her but I guess I did not do enough and this is where this story begins
Why do I feel responsible for her downfall when I did all I could to protect her entire world
We were at a birthday party at a friend's house and a boy slipped something in her drink and she haven't been the same sense
She would disappear for weeks at a time and my entire family would search all over the metropolitan area for her
First we called everybody we knew and if they haven't seen or heard from her then we would regretfully call the police

I have spent sleepless nights laying prostrate before the Lord and calling out her name until I lost my voice
A close friend of ours saw her walk up to his car and she made herself available for any and everything for money
He said he rolled down the window calling out her name and asked her when was she coming back to church
He told her that the pastor missed her and so does the church members but she only turned and slowly walked away
He said he prayed that God would step into her soul and renew her spiritually, mentally, and to free her mind from bondage.

"Letters from Jail Pt. 1"

Before I say a word, I already know what you are thinking and all of us have been in trouble. Being in jail for some people is a good thing because it blocks out the distractions, so we can finally focus on one thing. Who do you know is totally free and why do some people have problems with living a plain old ordinary life? What is living without expressions and why live in a world with walls, fences, bars, and mental institutions? This letter is from my private space and I pray these collective of words would free up our unlimited mentalities.

Having everything at your fingertips and being able to say intelligent things from your lips can make you feel free. Just because you have everything does not mean everything is okay inside of your world. Let me try to be more discreet or simply put measuring my statements in a clearer fashion or being politely careful. The rich are rich by what they have, and the poor are poor because of what they don't have. Do you have to have anything to be somebody or could you dive deep into your own imagination and imagine a different life. Having a job is like being in jail because you cannot do what you desire, and you must work for certain hours.

They have what you need, and they will hold it until you complete the necessary task assigned to you. Measure up and get rewarded but fail to fulfill their requirements and it will become just like being in jail. Being locked away in a confined space is not exclusively limited to correctional institutions. These spaces are in our homes, on our jobs, in our communities, in our religions, and deep within our own minds.

Everyone thinks of flying away to a place of peace and serenity, but few ever get there in the flesh. Why am I given such a miraculous gift and why did God set aside this time for us to think so intensely? It's two forty-five in the morning and I cannot sleep, as the spirit of the lord has me pinning this to encourage you to be free in your mind and spirit. God has a plan that is greater than every man and He will get his message to everyone who will listen. The only difference between me and you are our location and depending on that location determines our personal freedoms. Do not let your circumstance confine you.

I am free, and I honor God and be true to myself, then and only then can I attempt to deal with my fellow man, I am free to have what I have, and I pay the bills and even than there are rules, regulations, and laws that I must follow. I am free to smile only when it is okay to smile, and I am free to laugh if my laughter does not offend anyone. I am free to speak my mind if my words are cordial, and I am free to shout out loud only when shouting is permitted. I am free to believe whatever I desire to believe if my heart is satisfied with the outcome.

"Letters from Jail Pt. 2"

My prayer for you is that God would intervene in the spirit and start your complete healing from the inside out. Sitting in jail is a temporary situation and at some point, you must attempt to free yourself from your past. Nothing will change until God brings about that change, and you will be the first person to recognize the change. Change your mind and everything around you will instantly change because it starts first deep within your heart. I had to change who I was and into someone with the power to help anyone who would listen.

We all can see your situations, but that does not give us the right to exploit or belittle your issues. Help comes in many ways, but you must agree to accept their help. This time if something hurts be the first to say so and be honest with your family, friends, and the rest of the world. Living in this day and time people will search until they get your undivided attention. Everything has a price even if we refuse to pay for it, the choice is ours to walk away or sell our souls in the process.

Every bucket must stand on its own bottom regardless of how much stuff is put in it. Let us all agree that every ugly situation is hurtful. but within our pain we must try to maintain our sanity. You must learn to be strong and courageous when they want you to join something you know is risky, unhealthy, and illegal. Be the first person to admit your wrongs and just know within yourself that nothing last forever. Will the real you please stand up against anything and anyone that threatens your personal health and wellness.

We cannot treat every issue with the same remedy and every remedy cannot solve every situation. Some things cannot be resolved overnight because everything we have done has to be brought into the light. What has more value than our souls and when we take a closer look no one lives forever regardless of our wealth. The next time we agree to anything in private, we better think of how it would be viewed out in public. Unless we change our ways and try to become an honorable citizen there will be a next time.

We cannot turn back the hands of time, but we can make good use of the time we are given. It is a crazy person to jump out of a perfectly good airplane without a perfectly packed parachute. Every great idea we get is not worth the thought, but every idea is worth thinking of to measure its worth. Look at where you are right now, and would you believe you made a thoughtful decision to participate. Who could you blame other than yourself and why would you even try to blame someone else.

"Lift Up Your Heart"

Only you can inspire God to move on your behalf and if you are
not too tired could you lift up your heart
Look up and lift your hands up and please don't forget to open
up your heart and give it to God
God will take your heart of stone and turn it into a heart of flesh,
and you and I know that is a miracle
With a heart of flesh this life will be filled with joy and happiness
but a heart without a home is always sad
A blessed heart is a heart that loves at all times including when
the enemy is knocking on the door of your heart

Be strong young weary heart and step out of yourself and jump
into the power of God with the heart of a lion
Celebration is in order because the God you serve has kept your
heart through every test and trial
Having a healthy heart is a gift from God and thinking of His
goodness is knowing your heart is beating
When you thought it was all over the heart inside of your chest
pushed pass go and allowed God to show Himself strong
If you think God is not real it is a strong possibility that you did
not search for Him with your heart

How do you expect to overcome your diversity without a heart
that is willing to outlast every sinful test
The greatest power is not inside of your mind, the power you
need to walk on water is deep inside of your heart

From time to time your mind may suggest some things but your heart will never leave a solid spiritual foundation
Desire to have the heart of a lamb because a lamb has a wise shepherd to watch over them
Everywhere you go and everything you do there is a God who loves and cares about everything that concerns you

Humble your heart before God and from the debts of your soul He will allow you to speak of great and mighty things
When the fires of this life gets too hot don't beg for it to stop just increase the fire that is inside of your heart
Burning are those desires to see this world through God's eyes and to help my neighbor to see the power of God
We have the answers deep down inside of our hearts but what good is it if we don't share with them those things to come?

They saw you worship and praise a God that you cannot see physically but through your spiritual heart God is here
We have to be an anointed vessel sent from heaven who will tell the world about the goodness of the Lord
Heaven already knows the desires of your heart and when you yield yourself unto Jesus Christ He will bring them to pass
Who will call on a God without ears and who will look for a God that they cannot see and who will serve God without their heart?

From my conception God has established the beat of my heart and today I am lifting it up so that Jesus Christ could bless it
I cannot die until Jesus Christ touches my heart and I refuse to live without His Holy Spirit leading and guiding me
I am going to stay right here and baste in the presence of God and worship Him with all of my heart.

"Live In Me"

Song

Intro:
For I desire to worship thee,
Nothing I have done was worth lying at your feet

Verse #1
Lord, I am your child and Lord You know what I will become
I am truly not myself unless Your Spirit moves within me

Chorus:
Move through me
Speak through me
Witness through me
Lord, Lord, Lord live in me

Verse#2
The world thinks it knows me for only you; Oh Lord knows my
past, my present, and my future
Whenever they see me let them see you and whenever they tease
me forgive them too

Chorus:
Move through me
Speak through me
Witness through me
Lord, Lord, Lord live in me

Vamp/Bridge:
Don't let me go back to yesterday just turn my head up towards
heavens way and please Lord give me the strength to pray

Outro:
I can live because He lives,
I will live because He lives,
I am alive all because He lives inside of me

"Lord Save My Spouse"

I have a personal request sitting before the Lord of Lords and before the King of Kings
I know it won't take Him long to fill my request because He is the Almighty God
I worship and praise Him for all that He has done and I still have faith in God for another miraculous move
I am grateful to be called a child of the King and to be on my way to a place called heaven
I will bless the Lord at all time and His praises shall continue to flow from my mouth

My spouse is doing things that were not written in our wedding vows
We said yes to everything the preacher asked and we both bowed down on our knees and prayed for spousal unity
All of our family and close friends were in attendance; and before we ended the Holy Spirit showed up
Because of the God inside of me I refuse to backslide and walk against the will of God for my life
I have a Holy life to live and a God to bless for pulling me out of sinfulness

The Bible says the man who finds a wife finds a good thing
That same man then finds favor with God only after he loves a cherishes his own wife
They two become one flesh and their bed is no longer defiled

At first our days and nights were filled with joy and happiness and now they are filled with loneliness and sadness
Why do I want to scream when I know that God has heard my prayer

Half of my heart is happy with the past and the other half is confused because of the present
My heart is hurting because our marriage is on the rocks and the tide is rising above my head
Sometimes I am hungry for their affection but now I cannot trust getting a simple kiss
We are one flesh but I refuse to partake in anything that will jeopardize my future
God is going to get us through this storm and on the other side is a greater victory for our marriage

At first I blamed myself until I retraced my footsteps and God revealed the true meaning of our calamity
I feel so bad for my spouse because they are lusting after the flesh and all I can do is pray for their soul
What they have at home cannot be found anywhere else on the face of this earth
My love is reserved only for them because I vowed to love them through sickness and health
In reality I could be them and they could be me and at the end of the day we still have bills that need to be paid.

"Maturity Speaks Volumes About Our Character"

Wherever you go and whatever you do the only thing that will lift you high above the rest is your maturity
Immature people attract other immature people because they need someone on their level to associate with
Everybody will not receive proper instructions when they should and some never would
The only way the light gets turned on is somebody that is more mature has to turn it on
Your actions will tell the world exactly who you are and there is no hiding your level of maturity

There will be plenty of time to play your childish games after you get finished out smarting the competition
If it takes longer for you to reach a plausible level of maturity your generation will be light years ahead of you
Children don't know when to stop playing games because childish games have on recognizable boundaries
At no time do you have to disclose the inner workings of your mind, wisdom and knowledge is priceless

If you are smarter than the person besides you then you become their master

If you are equal to the person beside you then the two of you must decide who is going to take the lead
If you are uninformed in multiple areas then you will have to follow the orders of everybody else
If you refuse to follow orders then how do you think you are going to make a honorable living?
If you cannot make an honorable living then how do you think you are going to be honored in this society?

By not growing stronger and wiser you have placed yourself in a dangerous position
Where are you going to live and how are you going to eat each and every day?
Even if you died right now you're dead body will occur a bill that would have to be paid by somebody
Each of us are able to provide for ourselves and the only reason why we are not is because of a illness
You could have been way more than you are but you stopped the mighty hands of God from blessing your life
When God said to study you did not and when you refused to empower yourself the entire world is now suffering

What will you leave in this world that is valuable to this generation and for those generations to come?
The way this is looking God is going to use the next generation to instruct your generation on how to live
Because of me I cannot move to the next level and because of me everything in my life is in jeopardy
Here you come again with your hands out and what makes this so sad is you actually think you are entitled
The character of a beggar is less than the person inside of the body because a beggar has refused to use their knowledge.

"Mr. & Miss Self"

Ladies and gentlemen at this time I would love to introduce to some and present to others Mr. & Miss Self. People will appreciate you for the gifts you display, and some will be envious of your gift. People are selfish because they think of themselves first and anyone else last or not at all. God is the giver of all good and perfect gifts, so why are you pressing them for their blessings? Whenever you take who you are and give yourself totally to God the creator, then you can ask what you will.

Carry yourself to God and surrender for He is the only one who will never leave you nor forsake you. We have priorities to managed and minors to major for in this life everything has a purpose and a plan. What is your plan for today and are you planning anything for tomorrow, or what about your future? God has plans for you, but you refuse to listen to them and God has a judgment in your near future and you will not miss it. People will call you selfish for looking out for yourself, but in every emergency put your oxygen mask on first.

Who do you know is more dedicated to yourself and who can you call on when nothing is left on your shelves? We are only given so much time to succeed and the money we get must last for more than one day. Spend your money irresponsibly and denying your daily responsibilities will land you in mountains of debt. We all have needs and some of us are so greedy for who separates what we need and what we want? Secure your situations first before you reach deep into your pockets attempting to pay for theirs.

They will cry until you help them and then they will cry because you did not help enough. They cry when you were born, they cried when you graduated from college. They cried when you bought your first home and they cried when you refused to ride them in your new car. They cried when you denied their personal loan and they cried when you took the time to help someone else. They have cried and cried trying to gain your attention, your sympathy, and your affection.

Funny how they think tears will gain them access into your heart, your mind, your spirit, and into your soul. Hello Self, you have the right to speak your mind, cover your heart, worship God in the spirit, protect your soul. While they are begging you, they could be helping themselves to becoming more self-sufficient. People are helpers, takers, givers, or beggars, and others are thinkers, dreamers, visionaries, or procrastinators. Mr. & Miss Self; help those who need the help and bless those who are truly helping someone else, good day.

"My Faith Is In the Blood!"

Physically we have never met but spiritually we commune together each and every day
Before I close my eyes for the night and soon after he awakes me in the morning thank you are my choice words
The God who made me expects to hear his praises and the vessels he has made are yielded and obedient
Somethings my flesh desires to do but my faith in the blood of Jesus Christ wants my soul to remain whole
I cannot separate my soul from my spirit they both came as a package deal all the way from heaven

If I had the wings of a pure white dove I would fly away but until then my Lord wants me to use my faith
This world tries to conquer my soul by breaking me down like tiny specks of dust but first they have to go through the blood
Everything that goes through the blood is made whole and everything that the blood touches is no longer the same
I was sinking in sin without redemption and with one word of faith the powerful blood of Jesus Christ saved me

Some sins I really enjoyed doing and God knew it but with sin man cannot see the Lord

Give me the joy of the Lord and the blood of Jesus, and I will say good bye to this old world of sin
My fight is a faithful fight of faith and my hope is in a Sovereign God who can deliver me out of the hands of my enemies
As I pray for you will you pray for me and as I display my love will you return the same towards me

The enemy desires to come between us and cause divisions but our Lord has made that spiritually impossible
My prayer is that we remain faithful and not fail our missions for God, for there is a great reward now and in the heavens
You can because Jesus Christ is Lord and you have the victory because Jesus Christ said it was finished
This world cannot do no more to you than you allow them to but with the blood on your side nothing can touch you

I am more than confident in this and I am writing these words to increase your faith in the power of the blood
What else could I say except to keep the faith and to remind you that trouble cannot last always
Some of us will have the privilege to pray together but there will be many more that will meet me at heaven's gate
The faith they had is the faith we have and the victories they had are the same victories we will have through the blood
The joy of the Lord is flooding my soul and what I am experiencing cannot be totally described in words

I can do all things through the blood of Jesus and I have faith in the same blood that will carry me back to heaven
Good bye world and hello to eternal rest, the miraculous blood of Jesus Christ has allowed my soul to cross over.

"Not Finished Yet!"

Broken hearts and happy thoughts, endless tears mixed with smiling faces, this is the beginning of intricate thinking. If, we never start a thing nothing would become of our dreams. We may have visions to inspire us to try to achieve our dreams and desires. One more story to write, one more person to inspire, one more closed door to open, and plenty more books to publish. The more I dream, the bigger the stories are revealed. My friend progressiveness is a sure part of my imagination that bubbles from deep within.

They refused to open their hearts and write the stories God inspired them to leave on record. Whatever voice rings the loudest inside of your head is the direction you will follow. These words are spiritually induced and by God they will not go astray with no end in sight. What we say from our mouth comes from our minds and what we write with our hands comes from our hearts. The real you will shine as bright as the sun when you put on digital paper everything God inspires you to become.

When we sit and think deep within ourselves those thoughts are fresh off our minds and unlimited. What is the worth of your intrinsic thoughts and will they carry you to places only a brilliant person could go? Empower yourself literarily and never be left wondering whatever happened to your fabulous legacy. The smartest people will always have something special to write for they are thinking of today and tomorrow. These words are purposely selected to say whatever the author desires for words add true meaning to their questions.

When you cry out loud the world can hear and see your tears and when you write with passion we all are truly blessed. Comfort me with strong words and soothe my mind with words simply placed in an order. Take me on a ride I have never ridden and please include hills and valleys and an occasional bump in the road. Will there be potholes and speed bumps mixed with railroad tracks? Please don't include any dead ends streets? Some of your stories are so sad and others are forever exciting.

The smile on your face is priceless and the way we feel after reading your miraculous creations is truly memorable. Never have we ever read such a collection of words with love as the foundation and God having the final say. Words describe how we live, and they define what's right and tells us to turn around when we discover we are wrong. The words we read are directly responsible for who we are as individuals and they mold the things we do and say.
Thanks to all my family and friends for listening for only God knew how these words would transform our lives.

"On the Edge of Your Seat"

Laid back all because you got it like that and deep within your mind nothing else will change in your lifetime. Are you still alive and do you have the activity of your limbs? Why now when there is still so much more to do, and your own children are still depending on you. Take a walk and this time have a talk with yourself for there is a next chapter and a book with your name on them. How do you desire to be remembered and the way you are thinking your eulogy is going to be short?

What about, "What about?" Do they matter anymore or are you satisfied with the way things are going? You have longevity in your corner and if nothing else tell your story to the entire world. Make them hear every word you have to say, and you can always use the excuse that "it's your birthday". Tell them of the times you fell and got back up and then tell them of how God favored you above everybody else. As, long as you leave them excited and wanting more of what they came to hear then your job is done.

Sit up and pay attention for the competition loves it when you disqualify yourself and literally give up. This is about you and your family not about them and what they are doing in the earth. The seeds you have planted will come up and the harvest you are expecting cannot be cancelled. The home you truly desire to live in is being built and the car you always wanted is available for you to pick-up. The words you speak are your reality, and that is why a stranger cannot give God the glory for your story.

Your life is not over for you have more to do then to sit around and watch the world boast about their dreams. God has done it once and God is doing it again, and again, and again! Now what is your spiritual position? Everything happens in the spirit first and then God allows it to happen in the earth. Possession is one hundred percent of the law and with God working on your behalf nothing has the power to stop you. No man or woman, no job or career, no government or politician, no past or future, no illnesses or sickness.

Throw a party for yourself and let this world know you are not dead yet. Everything God has for you, is for you and the rest is for your children and grand-children. They wanted you to get mad at your children, so you would leave them nothing. Did you know their children are worse? They are the next generation and if the truth be told they are the recipients of your legacy. You don't know like I know what The Lord has in store for you, so sit "On the Edge of Your Seat!" with all expectations.

"Our Pastors Are Going Through"

We are living in a day and time when the trials of this life has no respecter of persons
The people that we think should have the power over certain situations are falling through the cracks
We have to continually offer up prayers to God the Father, Jesus the Son, and the Holy Spirit, who comforts us
The devil desires to sift the children of God as wheat; but that day will never come into being
Are you lifting up your pastor or are you allowing the demons from hell to use you to pull them down?

They have good and bad days just like we do but are we aware that they are still made out of flesh and blood?
They do sometimes stumble and if God don't catch them they will utterly fall
As long as we are inside of these earthen vessels there are going to be some occasions that we will have to fight
If the devil only comes to steal, kill, and to destroy what do you think our job should be?
You were hard as a rock while you were a sinner but how did you become so soft since you became saved

We need to stop judging them before we have all of the information and holding them to a unfair standard
Judge not so that you will not be judged and pray for them so that you would obtain the mercy of God
The same judgment we use on them will be used on us and by the way all have sinned and have come short of His glory
Where did you get your twisted evil thoughts and I dare to say you got them from the devil?
We are so glad you are so humble because God can using you to save the entire world

God has entrusted in them with the powerful Word of God and it is our duty to hold them up in spite of whatever happens
How long do you think we are going to stay on top of this mountain before we would have to go down to the valley?
Why would you put any human being on the same level as Jesus Christ when we are riddled with faults?
We are the ones who are searching for eternal life while Jesus Christ is sitting on high waiting for the call to crack the sky
While they are pumping up our spirits who in this world is praying and pouring back into them financially?

Please allow me to say thank you to those who are encouraging their parishioners to stay strong in the Lord
You could be the difference between them speaking life or death over the entire congregation
By you blessing them your blessing could inspire them to study another Biblical chapter and call on God the more
As the head blesses the body the body has the same ability to make the head even stronger
Remember they are still human beings and one day Jesus Christ will come back to take all of us home with Him

"Out of The Heart the Mouth Speaks"

If you did not already know your mouth could have life and death implications on your own life

Life and death is in the power of the tongue and we all have one

If you really knew the power you have over your own life at no time would you speak death over your own soul

Why would you desire to live a fabulous lifestyle and purposely speak death over my life?

You may be up today but what about tomorrow?

Every word that comes out of your mouth started when you formulated the thoughts inside of your heart

Either you are going to allow greatness to enter into your heart or you will embrace the evil that is within our members

How far do you think you are going to get by blasting insults out of your filthy mouth

You will have a greater effect with words that bless instead of using words that curse the people you call friends

If you are deficient in this area there are measures you could take to rectify your verbal situation

You are not as ignorant as you would have us to believe because you are very choosy about the words you speak

You sometimes mention your college experiences and we sometimes wonder why you have abandoned higher knowledge? The Word of God contains chapters that are filled with wisdom, knowledge, and a greater understanding
If that is not enough the dictionary is fill with honorable words and it also has the meaning of those words
Now the choice is yours as to continue down the road to destruction or to rethink the words that you chose to speak?

The same measure that we meet will be measured back to us at our individual judgments
This may be hard for you to understand but why is it so easy to insult another person?
This is just a plea from me to you and I pray that we all think before we speak words into the atmosphere
To some people this is a breath of fresh air and to others they could care less?
Warnings come before the judgment and this warning is no different

Change the desires of your heart and instantly you would change the words that comes out of your mouth
Listen to your thoughts before you speak words from your mouth
Could the B thoughts from your heart be more inspirational than your A thoughts that came from your head?
If you studied when you should there would be no problem speaking words of life whenever you speak?
Whatever you put into your heart will eventually come out of your mouth.

"Poison Running In My Veins"

The sun was beautiful and the birds were singing their same old songs, and would you believe I am still alive
Life is a gift from God and to take His gift and fill it up with poison is a sin
They said it would take me to a greater level but they never said it would cost me the later years of my life
Now simple task are hard to do and my body could shut down without giving me ample warning
Early this morning I wanted to move but my body refused because of years of drug abuse

Way back then my life was so simple but now the enemy inside of me has destroyed the vessel that keeps me alive
All I can remember are my mother's prayers and my father's strong hands of correction
They said no but I said yes they said don't take any control substances but I am such a disobedient child
As a youth I ran away from home thinking I knew a shortcut to success
My hands and feet are swollen from taking drugs and my organs are damaged from the lack of eating nutritious foods

Please pray that the next generation sees my faults and turn away from control substances
I will not see my grandson graduate from preschool and I spoiled the chance to teach him not to follow the crowd
Who will help me up and down the steps and who will save me from dying a horrible death?
There are still some things I desire to do but I cut the cord to experiencing happiness ever after
I am another great story with a tragic ending and when you read this I might have expired

I had a new truck and plenty of fine clothes to wear and I traveled in and out of state to the casinos
On the surface everything was grand but behind the scenes my sins knew me better than I knew myself
Before I could get out of bed those drugs had already planned my day
One hit to get up and another to keep my composure, and a stronger hit to fall asleep.
They would literally beat on my front door trying to wake me up but those drugs had my body comma toast

Why me and not somebody else and why did I fill myself up with drugs thinking I was doing myself a favor
Today, I have plenty of questions but no answers and on tomorrow I could take my last breath as your brother
Don't do what I have done and don't call yourself just having fun while doing drugs without a physicians prescription
You only have one life to live and if you destroy yourself then who will win?
When I die just place one flower on my grave and pray that the Lord would save my soul

"Pull Over and Take A Praise Break!"

Whenever you get weary in well doing just take yourself a praise break
If we weren't made out of flesh and blood we could keep on going and going
Time would have no place within our lives and our physical abilities would be unlimited
Some times when we get tired nothing else matters other than lying down and falling fast asleep
Are you like me a person who have failed to be strong in the mist of your storms and still refused to pray?

Even King David took out the time and encouraged himself and numerous times he prayed throughout the day
Go deeper inside Psalm 54, and you would discover a distraught worrier and a man who sought the Lord
Only when he took a praise break did he discover the miraculous power that our Lord had already given
King David moved according to the will of God the Father whenever a situation arose up against the Kingdom of God
All of a sudden the worried servant became a powerful Saint because he remembered how God had kept him

We are constantly making adjustments in our daily lives to ensure a maximum effort in all that we do and say
Some people want me to act like this and others demand that I act like them
A double minded person is unstable in all of his ways and I refuse to be that person
God gave us power and dominion over the things of this earth, He did not give us dominion over people
We can dance because God gave us the ability to dance and whenever we take a praise break we can dance for days

Stop trying to be a super saint and start being a child of God with the Holy Spirit living and moving on the inside of your heart
God knows when we are good or bad and God knows when we are happy or sad
The world desires to fake it before they make it but God wants us to praise Him before we see the blessing
Just to have the ability to lift your hands is a blessing and to open your mouth and bless His name is a miracle
I had to praise the Lord in spite of my issue, my situation, my sinfulness, my problem, and regardless of how I felt

When we fall into sin the Spirit of the Lord is still with us and after we finish He encourages us to ask for forgiveness
Never forget that the Spirit of the Lord is willing but these earthen vessels are weak and love the sins of this world
From the beginning we were never worthy of righteousness, it is only through the blood of Jesus Christ that we are not consumed.

"Read It Again"

It has come to my attention that you are reading words of knowledge, wisdom, and you're getting an understanding. Everything you hear is not worth hearing and everything you read is not worth reading, but everything about God is good! Reading to you should be fundamental, foundational, fun, exciting, informative, personal, and very necessary. When we seek God to guide us through his spirit, we will gain a greater understand. There are many books available to assist you in gaining knowledge. If it takes ninety-nine times to get an understanding, then read it until the doors and the windows of your mind are open

Seeing is often confusing but reading will allow your mind to obtain knowledge and your heart to eventually understand. I can write these letters because I have read words of life and over time all those words are now my intelligence. Judge me for the words that I speak and try me according to my actions, but never assume I'm not knowledgeable. We only know in part and we can only speak from what's inside of our heart. A slave will always refuse to read it for themselves, because they believe in their heart there is only one master.

Now you know why the devil was using people to keep you from learning. When you know what you need to know, the world around you must bow to your powerful and intellectual abilities. Every question they ask, you already know the answers and because you are highly informed nothing surprises you. Your tongue cannot speak without knowledge and your mind would fail you unless you fill it with specific information. Your world will come to life when you see it from Gods perspective.

Keep it with you everywhere you go and open it whenever your mind wants to know. Mark each page of highlights for those words will jump off the page and into your heart. Those words will become your character and your new character will shape your new personality. No one is successful without first reading words and be very cautious as to those words you allow into your mind. Let your words be life giving words when you speak to anyone including you.

The old is old for a reason and the young are young because they just started, but the question is who will you listen to? Some of us are fast learners, but after every storm comes a rainbow. I promise you this "The more you read the more you will know and the more you know wiser you will grow!" Inside of you are words of knowledge ready for recall whenever you are engaged in intellectual conversations. Always remember to be quick to hear and slow to speak, as we will give an account for the words that we speak.

"Shoes Off"

Have you not seen, have you ever heard the ground you are standing on is Holy ground? This is a warning to you and to the entire world, the earth is The Lords and the fullness thereof. Why are these things so for only God knows and it is because of Him we have life and have it more abundantly? Take a close look at your life and see the great things God has done for you. God is not like man that he should lie. He hastens his word to perform it! What he says he will do, it is already done. Let's give God the glory and honor he deserves. Let's thank him for his wondrous works in us and on the earth.

Take your shoes off and bow down before The King of Kings and The Lord of Lords. One thing I have come to know about my Lord is He don't play with sinfulness, disobedience, selfishness, or pride. When was the last time you closed your eyes and prayed out loud and made God proud to have you as His child? God loves us so much that he sent us a comforter and teacher. God will never leave us or forsake us.

When we worship God by lifting our hands and our hearts in complete surrender. We allow his spirit to lead us in his holiness. We cannot continue to take the God who created everything, ordained everything, and will judge everything, for granted. The devil is doing all he can while he can to distract you from ever experiencing the fullness of Christ. You don't know what you are missing and that is why I'm writing these words to pray that you will finally get it!

Some people have never humbled themselves before the Father or gave him the glory. Some people have not accepted the Son of God as their personal savior. Please make sure you are not in that crowd for their judgement will be swift and final. We have made plenty of mistakes in our lifetime, so don't make another by thinking you will get another chance. Try Jesus while you can, seek Him while He may be found, and never again walk on Holy Ground with your shoes on. I love you, but God loves you more, I care for you, but Jesus Christ lived, died, and rose again, for all our sins.

We can only witness to the least, the last, and the lost, for after that the rest is up to God. This poetic letter is giving reverence unto our God and these things we will do until He comes back again. Thinking of Him is a good thing and nothing on this earth can compare to His mercy and undeserved favor. Taking our shoes off tells God we honor His Holy Presence and we are yielded and still before His throne room. Anytime You desire to worship I'm ready to take my shoes off and when I worship things happen in my favor. God blesses me with his presence and for that I am grateful!

"Show Me the Other Side"

I heard you decree a thing and I heard you speak of thunderous faith but none of that is any good unless I can see the other side for myself

You have a lot of things and all of them looks great and the way you obtained them were by faith?

Some of your words I instantly understood but most of them took me into places I thought I never imagined

So faith are words that suddenly turns into a person, place, or thing?

I will believe in God because you have spoken so clearly and I will have faith in God because I heard it come out of your mouth

You said "The doors of faith are always open" and I say if you speak faith into my life then I too would have access

Faith without no man shall see the other side of prosperity but with faith through Jesus Christ all things are possible

God will do the miraculous when you use your faith in a miraculous way

You shall prosper and be in good health even as your soul prosper

Your soul must prosper whenever you are moving by faith because faith brings everything into existence

In these last days the people of God will move and think by faith; and literally gain access to the blessings of God our Heavenly Father

Count God in and He will never leave and by acting according to your faith the Spirit of the Lord would never fail
Bring Me a dollar and I will open the door but if you open up your heart I will open up the warehouse of prosperity
Because I waited on God to open up the heavens I can explain to you how the faith process actually works
God was not selfish with His blessings so why are you acting selfish when using your miraculous measure of faith?

The blessings of God are full and complete God has never started something and refused to bring them to pass
From generation to generation our God is so faithful and from our test far into our trials we are still being blessed
If we panic the Spirit of the Lord is not the blame it is because in the hour of the test we did not call out Jesus name
There is no failure in God and with Jesus Christ all things are possible; and it is the Holy Spirit that comforts us
My friend by faith you are already there and by faith nothing shall cause your faith in the Lord to fail

Over here the faith in Jesus Christ is greater than those earthy material things that we have asked for
You have not because you ask not but you could receive everything that your heart desires when you ask by faith
Never would you be able to eat a nutritious meal by eating at the vending machine
Only when you shop for the best and prepare the greatest by faith and then you will have everything you have said
If you want the best of everything then you have to pick up the Bible and study to show God that you are worthy.

"Some Are Happy Some Are Not"

Why is it that some people are happy about your progression in Christ and others are not?
I am not talking about my haters because I know their position but I am talking about my closest friends
Now I have to keep all of my visions and dreams to myself until they are revealed by God Himself
Would it be strange to ask God for something small when I could use my faith and claim the greatest of all?
The more I live on this earth the more unpredictable people become not strangers but family and friends

I have stopped trying to figure people out and I have started trying them by the Spirit of God
If you come to me and I don't think you are honest I have to wait to hear what flows out of your mouth
We live by the words we speak and by the things we think; thinking is a thought but our words are action
How come the level I desire in the Lord is never possible to the person on the other end of the phone?
I could appreciate the honesty of others when I can sharing with them all of my hopes and dreams

What has the power to stop whatever God has ordained?
If I said it out of my mouth then I believe God for it
Just because your faith is small does not mean that my dreams
are not possible
It is a normal reaction to want to share something special with
someone you love
It is not normal for those you love to display hatred and try to
share your dreams

Your true colors came shinning through when I desired
something bigger than you have ever seen
I believe Jesus Christ for the miraculous and when they come
true you will be the first to witness a miracle
When I mentioned the Bentley something changed in your voice
and you suddenly went on the offensive
Those cars draw a lot of attention not to mention they cost a lot
of money are the words you said
Not only is God going to do this He is going to bless me with more
than one, I am seeing at least three cars

As we talked I had the biggest smile on my face and I covered
the phone when I started to laugh
My faith wasn't even shaken by your faithless words but in fact
I actually drew greater faith in my God
When I mentioned getting another Ford vehicle you didn't say a
word, I saw through you like a clear glass
Well I guess you cannot enter into the promise land because you
have doubt inside of your heart
Every time you see me I will be higher in God and I do pray for
your strength in the Lord.

"Something Special Inside of Me"

Excuse me, why are you trying to pump up my ego, when I have seen my destiny years ago. This is the highest, I am permitted to go for I have deficiencies in many different areas. Like an unlearned person, I always revert into a mindset that hinders me from comprehending the truth. We each have a past that we had buried. Somethings aren't meant to be revisited. So, I'm asking you to leave me here to wonder about my future.

Are you sure it is me that you see something special or are you just playing with my broken heart? Hurting people, hurt others for they have hidden deep inside of themselves hurtful moments. I have been left alone and I had to build myself up again. I had to learn how to be me with masking the pain from my past. Now, you show up and speak life into me today for my tomorrow. You have activated heavens will for my life. The will of God is now what I seek after. I will listen for the voice of God and change my mind from being a loser into a winner.

The last time they spoke into my life, it hurt me because I did not understand the meaning of these words. I was above and not beneath, I am the head and not the tail. My weak heart could not comprehend this nor did my mind understand it. I had been promised, and lied too, so how can I trust you? Am I that open for a stranger to tell me when I need saving from myself? Words can give you life or used to curse your life. I'm tired of being the victim while seeing others be victorious.

I needed a shift, a change and I needed to hear from the creator God. God created me and gave me a new name, a new walk and talk. I'm rejoicing not fussing anymore. I have been lied to repeatedly, I didn't understand why. I had to pray for them, as my God has set up a great harvest for me in the next season. Unless you are speaking truth, I cannot hear or receive your words. There are many voices in the land, your voice, their voice and Gods voice. Gods voice is deep inside me and said that his children know his voice and will not follow the voice of a stranger. So, when truth is confirmed, it has a firm foundation. Truth will prevail over the lies.

"Stop Stirring Up Dust"

I truly hope you are having fun with the way you call giving a sermon
Only the Word of God has the power to wash my sins whiter than snow
You can preach until you are blue in the face and your words could not stop me from sinning
Faith comes by hearing the Word of God and the more you preach the Word the more faith I should have
By you bringing up my dirt is only stirring up dust and please tell me how that is going to help me?

We all are made of the dust of the earth and that is why we have to wash the dirt off of our skin
God can wash our sins away with His Holy Word but we have to wash our bodies with soap and water
Hygiene is so important to every person on this earth because all dirt can have a terrible odor
We will smell just by standing around and it does get worse while we are working
Don't take it for granted and never underestimate the power of the funk because all of us have issues

One part of me loves to waddle in the dirt and the other is trying to get back to heaven
Sin desires to overtake my flesh and cause me to ultimately miss heaven

There is a war going on without somebody reminding me of it but will they help me fight it?
God commanded us to love one another not to constantly bring up each other's dirt
Judging me is not going to help your situation but praying for each other will help our fight against sin

All that I have done and all that I will ever do will come back up at my judgment
You don't have to bringing it up God already has them written down in a book
Through the blood of Jesus Christ all of my sins are forgiven, past, present, and future
My fight today is to not willingly fall into diverse temptation and willingly sin against my God
I thought a person of your stature knew the ends and outs of the Word but I was mistaken

Thank God for the precious blood of Jesus Christ; His only begotten Son
Can you imagine this world without the Bible; now see how we are acting with the Word of God?
God has already made a way of escape but are we trying to use it before we fall into sin?
The Bible says to flee temptation and run into the presence of the Lord Jesus Christ in prayer
As many times as we have sinned why don't we make the next time a victory for the Kingdom of God?

"Striving For a Higher Plain"

From the beginning of time, unseen forces have been warring against the progressiveness of all mankind
A man may fall a thousand times but what makes him stronger is when he gets back up
We as a community cannot expect anything greater unless we pull together as one body for a greater cause
Out of the heart the mouth speaks and when our leaders open their mouths the entire body is blessed
God has blessed us with honorable leaders and we are charged to stand with them and to pray for them

We must glorify the God of all creation because He has heard our voices and He has answered our prayers
All that we are came from God and all that we could ever become is wrapped up in our leaders
Our choice must have a plausible track record and be honored in their community as well as at home
A people person is who they should be because the office they are seeking is public and not private
We have a candidate who is honored and respected; they are faithfully serving the community

The time is now and the choice is crystal clear; we as a community could make national history
Putting all things on the table and casting out all doubt; once more we will overcome all of the odds
There will be excitement deep inside of our hearts and political stability throughout the entire community
The voice of God has spoken and the Spirit of the Jesus Christ is moving on the hearts of the nation
By faith we are celebrating this victory and by faith our community will prosper and remain an Ark of Safety

The fight for freedom and Justice is short lived and with an anointed vessel sent from God we are victorious
Having them there to speak on our behalf is comforting to our spirits and peace to our souls
They have stood the test of time and now their legacy will continue to enlighten generations to come
Deep inside of my heart, I still believe that God is sitting on high and pouring out His blessings upon all flesh
Take this moment and shout from the top of your lungs for the joy and happiness that you feel deep within

Please allow me to leave you with some quotes from our past and present leaders
I have gone to the mountain top and I have seen the Promised Land.
I believe that every person is born with talent.
If you want to lift yourself up, lift up someone else.
Where there is no vision, there is no hope.
If my mind can conceive it, and my heart can believe it, I know I can achieve it.

"The Activity of My Limbs"

What more can I say but thanks and who do I give all the praise?
The one and only creator God who made all of this possible; without any assistance from mankind
Let there be no doubt as to who gets all of the praise and even now God gets all of the glory
You may think all of your strengths are at your command but why is it that one day we all are going to die?
The very thoughts that puzzles your mind are the same thoughts that solidify my faith in Jesus Christ

Falling down on my knees and offering up heavenly words of praise is my reasonable service
Having the strength to do all that I desire is never taken for granted because it could be taken in an instant
Just because your mind gives a command to your body does not mean that the body will carry it out
Have you ever been walking down the street and felt a pain in one or more of your extremities?
You have to know without the help of God, Jesus Christ, and the Holy Spirit, your life is not worth living

I can walk, I can talk, I can raise my hands, I can think for myself, and if I have any problems I can go to God in prayer
My personality is not one that is so evil that others around me cannot see The Lord living deep inside of me
I want nothing more than for all the world and God to see that I am truly grateful, humble, and thankful
May my actions be those that are pleasing in the sight of my God and towards others that are around me
Let me first say this before I become remiss and forget that I am still made out of flesh and blood and apt to sin

I refuse to complain about what I don't have but I will give a sacrifice of praise for what I do have
If you see me jumping for joy and my heart is overflowing and when you see me shouting out loud I know my Lord loves me
Every day of our lives we have to be ever so grateful for the activities of our limbs
If you don't believe me go down to the hospital and pay a visit to those who have lost one or more of theirs

There were no set schedule for those who are victims of failing health or an occasion of amputation
Never again would I act strange when I should be giving my God the praise
Nobody and nothing on this earth has made it possible for me to live such an abundant life
Whatever I am God made me to be and because He is so graceful I still can say I love His wondrous works
The closer you look the more you will see the powerful hands of God all over me
If I find it hard to speak and my emotions have peaked I will wave my hands to say thank you Lord for being so good to me.

"The Faithful Few"

We are living in the last days and I have noticed there are just only a faithful few
They show up early and they stay late, and when necessary they know how to take a break
Broad is the way to death and destruction but narrow is the way to life and peace
They are the peace makers, they are the true givers, and they are dedicated to the cause of Christ Jesus

You have to learn that this world is not your friend they will use you up and throw you out with the trash
They study the Word of God and when prompted they are accurate with their response
What could possibly be more important than the life that you're living for Christ Jesus?
They know when to speak and they know when to be quiet, they will only say what's correct out of their mouth
Being faithful is more than showing up it is what you do after you show up that makes the difference
Are you one of them or are you working towards becoming everything God requires of you

We are only given a short window to make our decisions and whenever we procrastinate our minds become more doubtful
Can God depend on you to work for Him and become faithful to all that He would have you to do?

Did you work for God in your teens, what about your twenties, maybe you did something in your thirties, what about your forties, it is not too late even in your fifties, how about your sixties, even in your seventies there is still a chance, your eighties could be the greatest, what about your nineties, even in your hundreds it is not too late

God has a job for you to do and if you are still breathing then God desires to use you

Back in the Bible days they searched for righteous men and in this day and time God is searching through this generation

Could you be counted as being faithful to God or does your lifestyle disqualifies you from holding the title

To be noted as being faithful is more than a onetime event this recognition is deeply in bedded inside of our hearts

Many have stood up only to be lead astray this walk has to be done in a very specific way

To make a declaration before men is one thing but to make one before God has eternal implications

Be faithful to God and to your fellow man and please don't forget to be faithful to yourself.

"The King of Common Sense"

What is the only thing standing between us that we all can understand, and that one thing is common to all men. Our language is the only thing connecting us and together as human's beings we can communicate intelligently. Thinking is a common gift given to every person but thinking progressively or commonly must be taught continually. Having lived for five decades and working as a professional my knowledge of things has advanced tremendously. When we are not high and powerful we must reserve our knowledge of things to maximize our energies.

Values are not automatically calculated, and morals will separate the fool from those who have intelligence. Everyone should have the common ability to put into words their hopes, dreams, and whatever they really mean. Once there's a written record of what's said it cannot be denied so what are you going to leave on your literary journal. Somethings doesn't require your God given gift to achieve because numerous things about you are common. Moving forward is common but turning around is not and having great morals is common but having none is not.

Think for a minute who you really are and now tell the world why you are not able to think for yourself? Every sense your childhood people have been trying to pour common sense into your immature mentality. I'm aware of the deficiency for some people to have a simple conversation and do you think that's common? Desiring to control another person is not a common characteristic but seeking the friendship of another person is very common. I think, and I am somewhat sure that I am the "King of Common Sense" and I welcome your honest opinions.

Often the greatest people in the world are never recognized all because they did not have riches and wealth. Who have had everything easy and sweet for things cannot make us happy for they only make issues more convenient. Like having a job money makes working easier and raising children without money makes raising them much harder. Money makes the college experience easier but paying back the student loans after you graduate is not that easy. I have never enrolled in the college experience but that has never stopped me from using my common sense.

Is bigger better or is being smarter makes you more intelligent for at the end of the day every man gets tired. Having common sense tells you to rest after working and having good common sense will make sure it happens. Common sense will inspire you to be all you can be even if that means denying yourself of some simple pleasures. What's common to me may not be common to you and having common sense gives everyone the opportunity to be excellent. Fighting for your right to become excellent is common and showing love to every human being is exceptionally common.

"The Smartest Small City"

There is a place not so far away and it is close enough to the District line that it feels just like home. Across this nation and around the world people are searching for progressive communities to call their home. You will know it when you get here, and your neighbors will respect you and your love for them will never grow old. You could reside in this small town and live in peace without feeling the need to pack up and leave. We are famous in many ways and with this status we love our city, cherish our state, and are grateful to live in this nation.

You may have traveled around the world and have shaken the hands of dignitaries, but have you been to visit our small town? We are closely connected to a prominent city that could is within inches from our backyard. It makes us prime real-estate, as location matters in this market. We, brag about who we are, and we won't for we do have a soul that our neighboring communities' desires to have. We have excellent community policing, a team that keeps our town clean, and leaders that are constantly dreaming. In the early 1900's they truly envisioned this day and now in the 21st century we are taking this "Small Smart City and turning it into an excellence" worldwide.

Within this "Small Smart City" there is a secret hidden deep within her walls and its high up in the cloud. What is it you may ask and how did it get there is our unwavering desire to inform the entire nation? She is literally smart to the core because of her ability to measure herself through analytics making perfect her goals. Without this "Integrated Operational Center" she would not have a heart and with it never again would she become lost. Ask her any question and she will answer and if you have time to spare she will never leave you in despair.

There are two branches of government the Legislative and the Executive in which they both guard over each other. Citizens demand of her excellence in government and deep within her soul excellence is her reality. Together we have survived many public and private storms so just hang around to hear our smart pitch presentations. Come along with us as we journey through the data processes and become "Smarter" in every way imaginable. Upfront and transparent is our command for we are moving into a model community worldwide as fast as the data reveals the truth.

Our citizens are modeled after their love of the nation and their ultimate goals are to live in peace and to leave a legacy. We have a power like no other and with it no one could ever manipulate us out of our hard-earned Dreams. My home is my greatest investment to date and because of it I am a home owner, a good neighbor, and a representative. As you go about your day make plans to visit our fair city and while you're here please patronize our businesses. Don't become a stranger, you will be welcomed from your very first visit. We are small smart city that loves it citizens.

"The Sounds from The Crowd"

The fans love the things I do, and millions applaud dearly after my gifts are performed. At each event, I never get the time to vent for the crowds are so loud they drown out my fears. My matches are so intense and every now and then I must scream out loud, speak my mind, or break my racket. My job is performed in the public and sometimes I wish my matches could be played in private. Looking at them I wish I could give them all the biggest hug and share with them how important they really are.

They sit with expectation as my love for this talent makes me proud while hearing them clap even louder. So much so I could not hear the score as I just finished winning a twenty-shot rally. The claps are louder and longer for the one who wins the point, and, in this sport, they applaud both players. It takes a strong mind and an enduring heart to play this sport and that's just to make it to the court. When you hear me screaming I'm trying to encourage myself and when I lift the trophy I managed to overcome the pressure.

Year after year I return to display my gift from God and the competition gets younger and younger. If I turned back the hands of time I would not have been the number one player in the world. Wow! What a ride to be on sometimes up and sometimes down and I'm sometimes picking myself up off the ground. I thank God for my box and with them I find hope and strength whenever I find myself down. Everyone needs love, and God is Love and we will bring Him glory.

Fanatics come early to every event and they don't mind staying as long as it takes for me to break my opponent. They sit in the hot sun without a care, but in between sets they scurry to the snack bar to get their favorite refreshments. Some people follow me wherever I go. I am appreciative of the love and support they show. I work extremely hard and make sacrifices in my personal life to ensure I can stay a head of the game.

Do you hear what I am hearing and are you seeing what I am viewing for I hear their loud applauses and I see the victory at the end of the game. Therefore, I love the centerstage so much, it is the place where the winner's dwell. I give God the glory and honor in allowing me to be victorious. Facing someone physically stronger is a challenge and most of the time they are statistically superior than I am. There is not an opponent that I believe will conquer me. I stand in faith knowing that the greater resides inside of me.

"The Struggle Is Not Over"

The more I desire all of my struggles to end the more I have to pray that God will keep me if I fell again
I am not as strong as I think but through the powerful blood of Jesus Christ I am already victorious
It feels great when I yield myself to the Spirit of Jesus Christ and to allow Him to carry me to safety
This flesh has a problem with obeying the will of God and remaining sin free is sometimes more than a challenge
The Word of God encourages me to lean on Jesus Christ and to surrender myself in the Spirit and to deny my flesh

One moment my spirit is standing strong but my flesh desires to go back to the place that Jesus had set me free
There is a war going on inside of my soul and it has been going on way before I took my first breath
Sometimes I am victorious over my temptations and there are times when my flesh wins the fight over my spirit
Because I have studied the Word of God for myself immediately after I have sinned I fall down on my knees and ask for forgiveness
Living with unforgiveness lying inside of our members sets us up for a even greater fight with the adversary

I have heard many songs stating the struggle is over when I have been falling in sin and only Jesus gets me up again
They are not telling the truth they only want to hear themselves on the radio
We are famous for running with a lie and calling it the truth
We love to water down the Word of God and when the truth is revealed we ask the Lord to forgive us for getting it wrong
Many will take half the scripture and form it into a lie and make it out to look like the truth

Our sins have been cast as far as the east is from the west and we should constantly thank the Lord for that eternal fact
It is also a known fact that we the saved in Christ are actually sitting in heavenly places
Whenever we have a peaceful moment in this world those moments came from the Lord Jesus Christ
There is an adversary who wants to make every day of our lives a living hell but they have to go through the blood
Unless we come to know the Lord in the power of His suffering we cannot reign with Him in His victory

Today I pray for the body of Christ and I am also fasting for the spiritual strength of every blood bought believer
Only the Lord knows our eternal fate and it is He who has given us the strength to stand each day
As long as we are inside of this flesh we are prawn to fall into divers temptation but just know there is a way of escape
If the Spirit of the Lord was not covering us with the blood of Jesus Christ we would sin and not think twice
Until we take our last breath we are going to have test and trials in our lives but the Lord has defeated them all.

"The Wealth of The Wicked"

Today I pray that everyone acquires the wealth of this world
but it is God who determines who gets what
The Word of God says the wealth of the wicked is laid up for the
righteous
To know this fact is comforting to the believer because we never
have to worry about material possessions
There are those persons who think they have it all and nothing
and no one has the power to take them away
It is not possible for our God to lie and if God took the time to say
it them it must come to pass

For years I have wanted some special things and when I saw
others with their stuff I never became envious or jealous
The Spirit of the Lord has matured my spirit in this area and He
has assured me of everything God has for me is for me
If I shared with the world all of my desires they would say I
needed several lifetimes to achieve them all
My desires are dipped in the blood of the Lamb and more than
anything I desire to spend eternity with Jesus Christ
My expensive homes and vehicles will turn back into the earth
but my soul will be at peace with the Lord

The earth is the Lord's and the fullness thereof and they that dwell therein

The sinner man cannot imagine the judgment that is yet to come and only the Lord discloses the truth about the future

Everything we have came into being for a purpose and everything we don't have cannot be accounted towards us

The adversary loves to accuse the brethren of worshiping idols when in fact God desire to bless all of His children

We are blessed so we could become a blessing to anyone who ask and we are to never deny their request

What I am about to say is the truth; the wealth of the wicked is laid up for those who are the righteous of Christ

Some of you may doubt this fact but that will not change the mind of God the Father

Whatever we sow we shall also reap and if we sow unto the flesh we shall reap those things of the flesh

When we sow unto the Spirit of Jesus Christ we will reap everything that the God of heaven desires for our lives

Appreciate the things of this world but don't worship them but rather worship the God who made all of these things

Please don't become alarmed I am not talking about taking any of your stuff because that would make me a thief and a robber

As a matter of fact I pray that you get all that you work for because soon and very soon I will have all of my desires met by God

At any given time we have to give up the things of this world because we came into this world with nothing and we are leaving with nothing

The Lord Jesus Christ is coming back to create a new heaven and a new earth; and then I shall have what was laid up

This life does not start with money and it will not end with money; this world exist because God the Father created it.

"Thirty Days of Fresh Flowers"

How would you like to have flowers delivered to your residence for the next thirty days?

All you have to do is to come home from work and they will be sitting at your front door

Each package will be clearly marked and there should be no mistaking as to who those beautiful flowers belong to

Please let us know right now if this could become a problem with you and your neighbors?

You do know when God starts blessing the devil will start to messing?

You can pick out any shape, size, or color, and we will handle the rest

We want this for you as much as you desire it for yourself and that is why the total cost is on us

Open up your heart to this great event and you will discover a miraculous change in your life

Change is good when it takes you to the next level because we all could use some encouragement every now and then

Maybe getting one flower at a time or having them presented to you in bunches just might bring joy into your life

Pretty will be the colors that fills your home and the sweet smell of exotic flowers will dominate the room
Take a sniff and you will instantly know that your world has changed without opening the window
As happy as this occasion could be your haters are going to look at this as a glorious day
They will send a very special bouquet just to say goodbye to the one person they hated all of their life
You have to walk out of your front door with your head up and walk pass them with the biggest grind

Never worry and never fret this flowery situation will last for the next thirty days
They thought you had died but to their surprise your entire life has changed for the better and not for the worse
You have reversed the curse and God has opened up heavens windows and He is pouring out miraculous blessings
Those haters will have to see you move pass the struggle and finally unwrap the gift of life
Delivered with a bunch of roses were a Holy Bible and inside of it is the keys to gaining eternal life

You should be happy to have had such a beautiful experience and grateful to God for giving you His unmerited favor
The world around you doubted your existence but the God of Heaven had faith in your ability to live again
A flower pushes itself out from the dirt and shortly after it blooms into something beautiful for all the world to see
This is your season for harvest but remember to plant your seeds in the spring to gather again another beautiful dream
Now that you are blessed with favor from Jesus Christ; don't forget it is better to give than it is to receive

"This World Is Not Our Friend"

If this world truly loved us they would have never treated us so cruelly

They will press upon you to do more than humanly possible and when you fail they are happy

As long as you have money they are sweet as honey but if the money runs out so goes the friendship

These issues you may not know of because you are so young, green, and so immature

Never worry and never fear the truth is here and without the truth you don't have any friends

A true friend loves at all times even when it hurts deep down within your soul

They will go to the end of the test and whenever this life gets confusing they will help you through your trials

Nothing hurts more than to think you have a close friend and to discover them to be an undercover hater

Some of us are blessed to have childhood friends for life and to share memories for a lifetime

If you have a great friend then treat them like they are closer than a brother

Why so many fights in the middle of the day and even more after the midnight hour?

Having to fight another person just to be respected is not friendship that is called bondage

The group that you are following is confused with living this life and with the pursuit of happiness

For once you should try being the leader and show them what real friendship is actually like

Now that you know what true friendship looks and feels like this bridge should stand for a lifetime

Whenever a person says they would always love you that could be a sign of their insecurity

Always is a long time to fake like you love somebody when you really don't

We live in a day and time when the divorce rate is higher than the marriages that are totally committed for life

How many true friends have you had within your short lifetime? Are you looking for a friend who would love you at all times or someone different?

This is one decision you will have to make for yourself and it is going to require your heart

If it doesn't feel right then it must be wrong but if it feels good then wait until they show their true colors

True love cannot be bought and real love cannot be taught; real love can only come from God

"Timeless"

Although you are not physically with us your legacy will always live inside of our hearts
You had the power to break down barriers and to mend every broken heart
Our lives are better because of your gifts and if given the chance we would do it all over again
Gifts are given by our creator God without repentance and we continually praise Him for them
The tears that fall from my eyes are for the good times and not for the bad; I want the world to know of your greatness

The first time I heard your voice my ears captured a sound that my mind had never conceived
Those words have life changing melodies and your voice was the sound that carried me over the top
Like a lifeless feather floating in the breeze your vocals moved me into a state of ease
Many have sampled your songs only to fall short of the measure God has given to you
I am not ashamed to tell the world I did the same and that is why I thank God for sending you my way

Song after song inspired me to reach for the sky and each one brought sporadic tears to my eyes
I purposely yielded my all while at the same time desiring to capture a sample of your miraculous gift

They laughed and they poked fun at me but deep inside of my overzealous heart I was serious
I song so hard and so long I lost my ability to talk which resorted in me using sign language
Please don't laugh my God given songstress has passed away and now I am at a loss for words to say

For the rest of my life I will have beautiful memories and a collection of songs that are timeless
We could only wonder did you enjoy your gift as much as we did?
Did you get goose bumps whenever you sang and are you nervous each time you grace any stage?
The first time I heard your healing voice I was celebrating a very special day in my life
Those moments are permanently etched inside of my soul; you gave me something I could never pay for

Last night was a repeat performance and I enjoyed it as if you where standing on stage expounding upon your gift
I am heartbroken because of your tragic passing and I pray now that you have eternal rest for your soul
We are morning over our lost and we have sent countless flowers to the place where you took your last breath
Even with this moment you have given us all the strength to overcome our almost impossible situations
Thanks for saying yes and for allowing God to sing those miraculous songs through your soul

God has graced us with a gift that will never be repeated and the world will always love their anointed voice
I followed you as your life unfolded on the television and almost every night I had my ear pressed to the radio

Wanting to hear every word that was song to perfection and also basting in moments of melodic bliss
To know that you were alive was comforting to my spirit but to know that you are deceased will be hard to fathom
The way I chose to say good bye is to play your beautiful music for the rest of my life

"Two Paper Hearts"

What could be more wonderful than to have two people sign their life away on a piece of legal paper
The world will never know the love that we have for each other
We communicated so much our different lives became too close to stay away from each other
The paper heart inside of me could not beat without her being in my life forever
Her paper heart were wrinkled and crumbled until I came along and added a fresh perspective into her life

The love I have for her is greater than a wedding ring and a paper contractual agreement
The vows we have made has become the target of the devil
We have to pray daily, fast and pray occasionally, and seek the will of God constantly
Through joy and pain, sickness and health, for richer or poor, happy or sad, even when we both are mad
Until death comes and takes as apart that is the only event that will change our hearts

You have to know that I am a real person with real issues and a heart that is full of dreams
On our wedding day we felt the joys of the moment and the love from our family and close friends
They had a wonderful time while helping us celebrate the love that God has joined together

Nobody acted out of character and everybody did the electric slide when the music started playing
At the end of the party we went on our seven day honeymoon while they went home

Our lives are intimate in our private settings and then on stage when we get out in the general public
People often wonder do couples really love each other and we are never afraid to show it
Love is something we do twenty-four hours a day and we recommend that every married couple try it often
Having a written agreement is what they require but having two hearts made of flesh is our dreams come true
Two paper hearts have become as one and on our first anniversary we will revisit every moment of our wedding day

One half of my heart is made totally out of flesh and never forget that the other half is on paper
Some marriages exist only on paper and each and every day they fake it like they are madly in love
I pray for theirs as much as I pray for ours because a paper heart could catch on fire and quickly burn up
Our love has grown larger than the paper agreement and our dreams together are bigger than life

"Up Chicago Way"

One of these old days we all will know why he went away but for now we are hearing of his greatness
Whatever he puts his hands to God is right there to multiply it a thousand times
There were no hesitation in his thoughts or actions because he was once a follower of one of our greatest leaders
Scholars took our now leader by the hand and taught him how to get results without losing the fight
He may have moved from his hometown but he understands how to live in a country and become bigger than his enemies

One man had a great opinion and another said it was less than his but why do we test our own freedoms?
We have the freedom to grow as intelligent human beings and to die with a great legacy
My mentor should have had the opportunity to establish his dreams in the place in which he was born and raised
If this is going to remain the land of the free and the home of the brave the people who live here has to stop discrimination
If they can embrace me as a laborer they should have the ability to accept me as their CEO

This man wanted to walk as another man but the another man wanted him to walk behind him
He never wanted to be like them but he desired to have the same opportunities as they had as human beings

Many times the odds seemed impossible and he girded up himself and walked as a proud child of God
They called them worse names and closed many more doors than they did stop their mentor
Scholars were assassinated and they said within themselves their life is not worth living unless he gave their lives for a greater cause

This man had gifts sent from God and with those gifts he did help to bring a greater change mankind
He went beyond the color of his skin and broke down those barriers that the past had posted as social barriers
Every time he opened his mouth the God of heaven moved those discriminations that made life almost impossible to live
Yesterday we had no faith but today we have faith, we give him double honor for raising the social contuses of the hopeless
He said "If we could believe it we could conceive and God knows we could achieve it"

I am one of his children because his words have helped me to see this world for what it really is
I am someone special is what he told me to say to myself whenever I am feeling less than my complete self
"If I can believe it then I can conceive it and because they said it then it must be true
We must honor them because they protected us and without them who would we be today
Be proud to be alive and to play a key part to making this world a better place to live

"Vessels Without Love"

Desperate times calls for desperate measures and when it comes to love desperation has no place
People have gone to ends of the world trying to find the greatest love and they have not found it
They have sacrificed their entire life and depleted their life savings only to end up unsatisfied
How could they find love when they don't know what true love looks like, sounds like, and feels like?
Can you see why they have never found true love and when we use collective reasoning they never will

There are billions of lonely people who are living with a false sense of where to find true love
They have multiple disorders and each one are only adding to instead of resolving their problem
We cannot eat our way and we cannot lust our way because Jesus Christ is the only way
We cannot talk our way and we cannot buy our way because Jesus Christ is the only way
Please note the vessel that surrenders to the Spirit of Jesus Christ can and will find true love

If you want to do anything great try doing it through the love of Jesus Christ
If you desire to leave a great legacy then build it on the foundation of Jesus Christ

If you want to be loved unconditionally and blessed eternally try Jesus Christ first and the rest is history
If you desire to move the world and show them true love then seek those things that are from above
If is a question but when is the answer and whenever you are ready Jesus Christ will show you true love

John 3:16,
God so loved the world that He Gave His only begotten Son and whosoever believes on Him shall be saved

God loved us before we loved ourselves and that is the greatest love this world will ever know
God sent His Son into the world and the world received Him not but that did not stop God from loving us
God moved through His Son Jesus Christ in the flesh to show this world how great His Agape love really is

There is no greater love than the love Jesus Christ has shown and for eternity there will be no greater love
Perfect love cast out all fear so why fear when the Lord Jesus Christ is here
No relationship is safe without the love of the Lord covering it with His miraculous blood
In the Lord Jesus Christ there is perfect love and if you want the greatest God has sent heavens best
The Lord has never lost a case and His love is wrapped up in His amazing grace

There is one who promised to have the greatest love ever but the end thereof is death and destruction
At first it feels like the real thing and deep inside of your mind it is so convincing

As time slowly pass us by it is so evident as to who the author really is, and it becomes crystal clear it is the devil
Look back and count how many times you thought you had found real love only to uncover the devil
Talk is cheap and true love cost something and Jesus Christ paid the full price for our love

Why would anybody give their heart to a person who does not have the ability to deliver?
On our best day nothing we could say out of our mouths would make us worthy and that is the truth from God
I love you once, I love you twice, and I love you with the only love that have stood the test of time
Have you heard of superficial love and how it could deceive the very elect of God?

You say you desire the purist love men have ever known and your desires could be fulfilled today
I pray that I have encouraged you to seek the love of the Lord and to finally obtain true Agape love
Search the Word of God and discover for yourself all of the many ways God has and will continue to love
Without love we cannot be called the children of God and that is a title that is worth shouting from the mountain top
The Agape love of God can be seen and affirmed only when you give your heart to the Spirit of Jesus Christ

Dance when you know how much God loves and shout when the Holy Spirit confirms it through Jesus Christ
Having love inside of our hearts is not an option but if you look closer it is a commandment

God commanded that we love one another and the Word moves to say that we love our enemies
Anybody has the power to love their own friends but can you show love to a perfect stranger?

How great is the love you show towards your neighbor or is that fact nonexistent
Love plays a greater role than we think and it is so easy for us to miss the mark
It took a Sovereign God to orchestrate an earthly plan in heaven just to redeem sinful man with His wondrous powerful blood
There is a Heavenly Father who sits on high but His love reaches all the way to the earth below

"What's in a Kiss?"

In some culture the first embrace includes a kiss and depending on where you are from it may include two. They have deeply embedded into their hearts the act of embracing, this is not the way everybody sees their neighbor. Get out of your country and you will see exactly what I mean for there is love being shared around the world. Just because your community will not participate in these simple pleasures, it does not create a barrier between others. Would you rather have a kiss, or would you prefer not to kiss and whatever you decide is your prerogative.

Who will you kiss today, your spouse, your children, or your friends, or will you simply keep your lips to yourself? This could be a private or a public matter but either way please make sure there's a mutual consent. Remember people have gone to jail for less and once your name is smeared all over the news you're then labeled a scrooge. Try a simple handshake and then allow a conversation to ensue before you go in for the kiss or kisses. Everyone is not as friendly as others, so we must be cautious when dealing with friends, family, and strangers alike.

The last thing we are doing is kissing for a kiss means way more than a simple kiss. Wars have started because someone refused to kiss, and peace was established because someone did kiss. This kissing thing is powerful and my advice to you is to never kiss anyone unless you really mean it. This kissing thing started as kids and has escalated into something unbelievable, unimaginable, and unpredictable. He kissed me, or she kissed me and either they liked it, loved it, or they hated it, and now you are in trouble because of it.

Judas, kissed Jesus for that kiss sent a message to the enemy of who was The Messiah. When we kiss it is more than just a kiss for it sends a strong message to those involved and to everyone watching. What is the last thing they do during a wedding ceremony? What is the last thing we do before departing from our love ones? What God has joined together may they forever stay together and kiss each other because they are now soulmates. If, you don't kiss then you were not that close but when you do the world can see your personal intimacy.

Trouble don't last always is what I have always said but that depends on who you have wronged. People have sued each other over a kiss and why you may ask for the answer is clear "We are not that close! A love song could have you all excited about the act of kissing but that is not the way everyone sees it. You better calm yourself down and keep your lips to yourself or else a lawyer will be serving you a summons. It's just a kiss you may say but they do have a right to say no and no means "NO!".

This is a good one and I hope you enjoy it as I truly enjoyed writing it. Come go with me to a place many will never venture and before we get there we must brush our teeth. Your smile is often the first thing another person sees and if your smile is twisted then you can forget a kiss. Our personal hygiene is always important and personally that says a lot about who you are. Okay, let's go in and explore a little more and hopefully in the end we will finish with a big kiss.

"When the Head Is Sick"

Only God could mend a broken situation and turn it into a blessing when somebody has spoken a curse over it
Everybody should seek the guidance of the Holy Spirit whenever we desire to be led by another person
When the head is speaking death over its own body God cannot intervene unless the words are regretfully confessed
Death and life is in the power of the tongue and the tongue is located inside of the head
The body cannot go any higher than the head and if the head is sick then the entire body is sick

They may have meant well but God has a set plan for the entire body of Christ
All the thoughts come from the head and if the head is not thinking then who is guiding the body
If a light bulb wants to shine then it must be plugged into a source that has the power to make it glow
The head of anything cannot be or do as they please; it is the head that leads the body down on its knees
If the body is not willing to change the head must not be as strong as previously thought

It is the head that suggest or commands the entire body to conduct itself in a certain way
Whenever the body moves the head has given it a command and if the body rebels the head must try again

All of the members of the body take direct orders from the head and when the head is not informed the entire body suffers
The head tells the feet where to step and it is the head who commands the arms what to grab and what to hold on too
If the head did not think of it the body could not perform it and if the head said stop the body has to stop

The body does not determine the definition of a word, that information is exclusively stored inside of the head
The head can only think of the difference between a thought but out of the heart the mouth speaks
The head often times thinks of the wrong conclusions but it is the heart that keeps the entire body stable
Out of all the fruits of the Spirit self control is the least mentioned but it is the most significant
The head cannot afford to stop praying because through prayer God hears the desires of the heart
A head without a body is something straight out of Hollywood and God had nothing to do with it.

"Where Are The Virtuous Women?"

As a man I have asked this question over and over again and I were directed back to Proverbs 31
What is so special about the Bible that it makes sense out of total confusion?
My relation with a woman is totally my business so then why is the Bible raising a higher standard?
Unless I search the stars for my wife my efforts are worthless because she is sitting in heavenly places
If my sincere heart does not go pit tar patter my mouth is going to remain quiet

The lady of my life must be full of the Spirit of Jesus Christ and not confused about her purpose in this world
She has to come into my world and make sense out of every last one of my dreams
I have a wish but she has all the answers, I have a desire but she is the reason why I want to live to see tomorrow
I am the master of my domain but with her we can become fruitful and multiply
She has to know that I am looking for her because deep inside of my chest my heart is about to burst

She has her seeds in the ground and her hands lifted high above her head with the praises of the Lord upon her lips
She is a worshiper of all of heaven and a giver to the God who made her bountiful harvest possible
She has studied the promises of God and each one of them she is thanking Jesus Christ for them
She cannot put her trust in any man because he is not her best friend, her husband, or her lord
She knows when to say yes to my approach and she understands why she has to say no to anyone who is unequally yoked

What other than God could hinder her work because she has confessed and believed in the God of all creation
All of heaven is working for her good when in her past a man such as myself made her walk more difficult
Could I have pushed her into the church with my uncontrollable tongue and a body searching for lustful events
It is all my fault and no one else but God could have sent me to her but I in turn ran her greatest love away
A man has to act like a man only when it is necessary and not when he is speaking to the love of his life

She is hid in God through Jesus Christ and if I desire to find her I myself have to be committed to the cause of Christ
My search has been redefined because of the tragic relationships of my not so distant past
I thought I was in love but that was according to the flesh and not because I were sold out to the Spirit of Christ
All of my actions caused more and more confusion as we both thought we were doing something new
Today I pray before I say hello and after I have opened my mouth the rest is up to God.

"Written Impressions"

May I beg of your attention and I promise to care for your thoughts like each one were my very own
With these words I desire to speak life into existence and to leave you with a written impression
I have the power to impress upon your thoughts and to leave a valuable mark
If, I don't walk in my calling I would be disobedient unto the God who called me to be a change agent
Some written impressions will reduce your faith and there are those that will increase your ability to seek the Lord

I know your time is short and your life is in the fast lane but all I want is to tickle your beautiful mentality
My gift is designed to encourage your present state and to inspire you to reach far beyond your faith
To become content is the will of God but God wants us to use our faith to get to the next level
I know you are highly informed in your worldly affairs but I am here to warn you that God desires to know you intimately
Out of the heart the mouth speaks and the things you have been speaking are not pleasing in God's sight

Having our minds spiritually stimulated is one of the wonders of this world because some people think they know it all
It is the creator God who stood out on nothing and spoke this world and the rest of the universe into existence

Then God said His Holy Word will not come back to Him void and
that was before a man had the ability to speak
The Lord has used chosen vessels to write His Holy Word and
each person were inspired by the Holy Spirit
God could have used anybody to carry out His command but He
chose to use an ordinary man

The only way you would recognize what I am saying you have
to know how the read written words
Many will never know the total will of God for their life because
they had not the ability to comprehend His Holy Scriptures
The wisdom of this world will be as nothing before God but His
Holy Word will stand forever
We have to study more than the words of this world because they
are temporary but `The Word's of God are eternal
We have not because we ask not and there are those who have
because they properly comprehended every word

At the end of our journey we will be so happy to have learned
how to read and to articulate God's creative thoughts
The Word of God filled our belly with rivers of living waters and
those rivers turn into streams of righteous words
The Lord deeply expressed Himself in Word and by deed; and
even today His examples are guiding lights to all generations
Now we see why so many people have fallen and are without
hope they did not take heed to their instructions note pre note
We can still turn to them and learn of Him for His yoke is easy
and His burdens are light

"You Are Going To Love the Way You Feel"

Right now you cannot feel it but in the future you are going to love the way you feel
Everything about you will change and within the process there will be some pain and suffering
In order to complete your total transformation God will not entrust your heart to anyone else but Himself
As you seek you will find, while you are knocking the doors will open, and before you ask your prayers will be answered
Never mine what they said about you but hear every word that the Holy Spirit is specking into your spirit

Sometimes you may not understand and sometimes you are going to get hurt in the process but never stop trusting in God
The way I see you and the way your enemies sees you are totally different, all I see in your future is unmerited favor
Be blessed my son and keep the faith my daughter for all that I will do through you cannot be measured
They said you would never recover but I say you will never get into any trouble
Miraculous are the works that will come from your hands and the more you trust in God the more you will understand

Every time they said no God said yes and every time they doubted your calling God called you blessed
Every time they dug a ditch God filled it up and every time they caused you to stumbled God was there to pick you up
Every time they hindered your steps God set your feet back on the beaten path and then made them even greater
Every time they talked bad about you God spoke great things into your future and they all will come to pass
Every time they hated on you God was there to love on you and His Agape love is more than enough to keep you

Now that you know all things are working for your good doesn't it feel great?
We don't base all of our victories on our feelings but we do know our fate by the written Word of God
Those who don't know the end before it ends have not studied God's Word in the beginning
I have read the Word and the Spirit of the Lord spoke clearly to my soul, now I have to pass it on

Why panic when God is in total control and why doubt if your faith is in our Lord and Savior Jesus Christ?
I would lose all hope if I didn't know God was real and I would feel mad at the world for treating me so bad
People who have no salvation has nothing to hold on to and now you see why they hate you
God wants us to love our enemies and to pray for those who despitefully use us, now what are you feeling?
God has a way that we cannot go under and God has a way that we cannot go over; we must come in at the door
You should feel better because of Jesus Christ; you now have total access to all of heavens best.

"You Are Inside Of My Dreams"

The place of your dreams has come into reality and has landed deep inside of my heart
How does it feel to be deep inside of my thoughts and now that you are here you will never be lost
Daily we bow down on our knees and pray to Jesus Christ the Lord over the heavens and earth
Worship is what we do and praise is our duty for our God has not left us to die in our sins
Once we thought in part and now we know the truth about Jesus Christ the giver of all life

There is a place far, far away that the pure in heart will inherit, by the blood of the Lamb and by the words of their testimonies
How wide is it only God knows, and how deep is it Jesus Christ has never told but heaven is connected to our souls
Our dreams have connected because the Spirit of the Lord has come to usher us back into heaven
Since sin contaminated our vessels this world were our home, but today we thank our Lord for saving our souls
This is a dream that you never want to wake up because it is the beginning of our eternal story

I desired to be carried far away from this place and into a place that no man had ever seen
Goodbye cloudy skies and hello streets of gold; goodbye sin and hello the righteousness of Jesus Christ
Truthfully I am ready but first I have to tell the Salvation story to as many people around the world
Are you living inside of a dream that no man could explain and only the God of heaven knows your name?
Just because God ask a question does not mean that God does not have the answers?

Over there is peace that surpasses all understanding and joy that flows mightier than any rushing river
Over there a day will never end and we shall drink of the fountain and never thrust again
Over there are treasures that the thief cannot steal and the love of Jesus Christ we will always feel
Over there the streets are made of gold and our eternal love for our God would never grow old
Over there our dreams will become a reality and we will worship the King of Kings forever

Constantly I dream of a place called heaven and someday I will sit at the feet of my Savior
This is why I purposely love my neighbors and pray for those who despitefully use me
Every now and then I have to turn the other cheek and I pray to God to forgive those who trespass against me
Because of our earthen vessels we will have some tribulations and some moments of confusion but the Lord has overcome them all
Now that you see what I see and you have dreamed what I have dreamed; go and tell the world the Lord is the King of Kings.

"You're Hooks Where In Me"

Because of Jesus I cannot get away and because of Jesus my life
is greater than I could have ever expected
Why didn't I jump off a bridge and what kept me from calling it
all quits?
Somebody had to have prayed for me and set up a Spiritual
barrier that the devil himself could not penetrate
I never saw the hook that was underneath the bait and when I
took a bite out of this world it almost killed me

The devil thought he had me hook, line, and sinker, but the
power of God freed me from the hands of the enemy
You name it I did it but when asked I did not do a thing
I was your classic liar who always denied the crime and confessed
to never being involved
Telling lies became a natural habit but when I told one I had to
tell another to cover up the first untruth
I have discovered through Jesus Christ it takes less to tell the
whole truth than it takes to tell a horrific lie

When the devil said to dance I danced and when the devil
wanted me to curse I opened my mouth and blasted off
Like a dummy on cue I made moves that satisfied them when
Jesus died so that I could glorify only Him

Each and every day it is God who gives me the activity of my limbs
If anybody knew these facts it should have be me because I was born and raised in the church
Back sliders like myself have a problem when it comes to making confessions about what I had done and who I done it with?

Thank you Jesus for coming into my life and now the hook called Salvation has taken full control
This world had me fooled to believe that my life consisted of things; they really had me blinded
Materialistic things have come and now they are gone but the love of Jesus Christ has changed my entire life
There where hooks in their fortune and fame; because their hand claps cost me more than I could ever pay
I want to be loved, I desire to be hugged, but I am not willing to sell my soul

Lord stay inside of me and never let me go back to the places that I loved before
Strengthen my mind so I can think of Your goodness and cover my heart so that this world could not destroy my soul
Guide my feet to the place that I first believed and teach my hands to reach up towards heaven
Permit Your righteous Words to flow from my lips and be the lamp unto my pathway so that I would not trip
I once were hooked in sin but now I am hooked on the Holy Spirit that lives deep down within my soul

"Your Greatest Desires"

It is a known fact that whatever you say out of your mouth has
earthly and heavenly implications
Man shall not live by bread alone but by every word that proceeds
out of the mouth of God
Say the wrong words and you will get what you deserve but say
the righteous words and be blessed by God
How much of God's Holy Word do you have inside of your heart
because out of the heart the mouth speaks?
You can ask God for the world but if it isn't His will for your life
it will never happen

Could you already have everything you have asked of the Lord
because that is your measure of faith?
Faith comes by hearing and by hearing the Word of God, now
what and who are you listening to?
Everything you desire the devil desires that you never receive it
and that is especially true about Salvation
Nothing in this world is more valuable than your soul and if
nobody else knows that you should realize the truth

As long as you desire stuff you are putting your soul in jeopardy
of falling into a fiery pit
Have you prayed with all earnestly and did you speak specifically
your request unto the Lord?
You are the only thing holding up your miracle because God is
still ready, willing, and able

This time pray the Words of God and keep out those desires that concerns the flesh
There is a great separation between heavenly blessings and the tangible things of this earth

God is not going to bless you with something that He does not approve of
Have you moved from where you are to where you desire to be?
Close the door and throw away the key and because of your prayers if God is who He is then another door will open
Why would the Lord Jesus Christ fail you when He has given His life just for you?
The request is upon your lips and the move of God is ready to take you to the places you have never been

Before you formulate your thoughts God has already fulfilled your request
Does everything around you still look the same and do everyone you meet still know your name
You will discover a greater lifestyle when the people you meet are not from your old neighborhood
Now you know another door has opened when everything around you does not look familiar
A test is an event that has not been revealed but as you take it the answers become easy because you are maturing
Great is the faithfulness of God our Father and great is your legacy because of your heavenly desires.

Printed in the United States
By Bookmasters